START YOUR MUSIC BUSINESS™

HOW TO EARN ROYALTIES, OWN YOUR MUSIC, SAMPLE MUSIC, PROTECT YOUR NAME & STRUCTURE YOUR MUSIC BUSINESS

VOLUME 1, MUSIC LAW SERIES™

BY ATTORNEY AUDREY K. CHISHOLM

Get the "5 Streams of Royalties Your Music Should Be Earning" Chart

Free by Signing up for our Mailing List at:

www.StartYourMusicBusiness.com

DISCLAIMER: This publication is designed to provide competent and reliable information regarding the subject matter covered. However, it is sold with the understanding that the author and publisher are not engaged in rendering legal, financial, tax or other professional advice. Laws and practices often vary from state to state and if legal or other expert assistance is required, the services of a professional should be sought. Similarly, some information may be out of date even upon publication. The author and publisher specifically disclaim any liability that is incurred from the use or application of the contents of this book. Every effort has been made to accurately represent the potential of the advice contained within this publication. However, the author cannot and does not guarantee any degree of success as a result of the following advice. As with any business endeavor, there is no express guarantee that you will achieve specific results.

DISCLAIMER: The professionals or companies referred in this book are not employees or agents of Audrey K. Chisholm or Chisholm Law Firm, LLC. It is entirely up to you to enter into a direct contract or otherwise reach agreement with a professional and we do not guarantee or warrant their performance or the outcome or quality of the services performed. Should you have a dispute with the professional, you must address such dispute with the professional directly. By accepting any referral referenced in this book, you hereby agree to release Audrey K. Chisholm, Chisholm Law Firm and its officers, agents, and employees from any damages or claims arising out of or in any way connected with disputes and your dealings with the professional.

Table of Contents

Acknowledgements

I would like to thank God for this incredible opportunity to share information for the benefit of others. I would also like to thank my loving husband, Dr. Juan P. Chisholm, for loving me unconditionally and for being my inspiration. I love you with all of my heart!

Dedication

I dedicate this book in loving memory to my late grandmother, Gladys B. Turner (1925-2010). Your legacy lives on through the many lives you have touched – including mine.

Giving Back

A portion of all proceeds from book sales will be donated to 501(c)(3) charitable non-profit organizations to support education and entrepreneurship.

Why You Should Read This Book

Y ou are a talented musician, artist, songwriter, or producer and the only thing standing between you and achieving your goals in the music industry is the right information. You know music, but you may not know business – or at least you have questions. You need to know the legal aspects of starting a successful music business and how to avoid being sued. You need to know how to fully own your music and masters as well as the rules regarding using other people's music. You may have heard information about protecting your brand but really aren't sure how to get it done the right way (copyrights v. trademarks). You know you should be earning royalties but need to understand how much, how to qualify and how to get paid what you deserve. You know there are laws and rules you need to follow but no one ever takes the time to explain those in plain English. If you've ever had any of these concerns, then this book is for you.

My reason for writing this book is simple. I am a successful full-time practicing attorney and owner of my own law firm. I have been fortunate to represent musicians, songwriters, artists, bands, record labels and producers. Many of them had incredible talent yet did not understand how to leverage business and legal principles to grow their music businesses. I found that they all had the same questions about business and law.

I began working them as clients and helping them structure their music empires in order to help them achieve their goals. As a result, my clients include record labels, songwriters, producers and artists whose works have been featured on MTV®, American Idol®, VH1®, Oxygen Network®, NFL® commercials and more. I have negotiated major recording deals with companies such as Disney® and have spoken to audiences of over 13,000 people around the country.

I am passionate about empowering talented musicians, artists, songwriters and producers because I am a musician. I have performed all over the world, but chose to pursue my love for business and law instead of a career in music. As a result, I understand the advantages major record labels and industry executives have due to their access to strategic legal and business advice through lawyers such as myself. I believe that musicians, artists, songwriters and producers should have access to the same information. I enjoy bridging the gap by communicating complicated legal and business concepts in a simple and easy to understand manner.

This book will not teach you how to write a hit song or how to become a great artist. However, it will equip you with the business and legal information you need to know to legally start your own successful music business in order to achieve your goals.

Feel free to e-mail me your questions, comments and thoughts throughout this journey at **Audrey@StartYourMusicBusiness.com**

Chapter 1:

Start Your Music Business

HOW TO STRUCTURE YOUR MUSIC BUSINESS

L et's start with some good news. Believe it or not, you've probably already completed the hardest part of running your own music business. The hardest part of running a music business is developing "you". That's right. You've probably already had some success developing yourself into a talented music producer, songwriter, or artist – or maybe all three. You may have already written some songs (or even sold a few), performed in front of a live audience, or produced some tracks. This book isn't about developing "you" or the talent you need to succeed in the music industry. You'll need a different book for that. Instead, this book is designed to help you understand and establish the legal and business aspects of your music empire. This will help save you money, help you make money, and help you protect your hard work for years to come.

The first step in establishing or structuring your music empire is deciding what type of empire (business) you need in order to accomplish your specific goals in the music industry. Believe it or not, business entities (corporations, partnerships, LLCs, etc.) are similar to cars. They are all generally built the same – but each one is designed to do different things. For example, to build most cars, you need an engine, transmission, wheels, and other parts. However, luxury cars are designed to accomplish a different purpose than race cars.

The same rule applies with business entities. It is a very similar process to setup a corporation and a limited liability company (LLC). Both of them require filing certain paperwork with the state. And it is a very similar process to register that same business as a record label or production company. However, the main difference between the business entities is that they are designed to accomplish different things.

Therefore, your first step in starting your music business is to decide which type of business you need to setup for your music business. This information is important even if you have already setup your business because you may learn that a different entity is better for your music business. If that is the case, rest assured that in most cases, you can change to a different one. So, here are the most common business entities (ways to structure your music business):

1. Sole Proprietorship

2. Partnerships (General)
3. Limited Partnerships
4. Limited Liability Companies (LLCs)
5. C Corporations
6. S Corporations

Sole Proprietorship: Risky Business

Let's start with sole proprietorships. You may already own a "sole proprietorship" music business without even knowing it. A sole proprietorship is the easiest and fastest way to start your music business. It does not require you to file any formal paperwork. It simply requires that the business have only one owner. You can use your own name as the business name or use a trade name (alternative name) by registering a "fictitious name" with your state (we will discuss how to do this later).

If you are an artist or musician and you are currently being paid to perform at local events, you may be considered a sole proprietorship even though you never registered your business as an official company.

Example: Justin produces music using studio software in his apartment. He has a YouTube® page with samples of his music and markets his business by writing posts linking to his music on Facebook® and Twitter®. Whenever friends buy a beat, he sends them a PayPal® link and they submit their payment to "Justin Rivers." In many states, Justin already has a legal business, known as a sole proprietorship, even though he has never filed paperwork with the state or registered his company.

However, even though it's easy to start, a sole proprietorship is also often considered the most dangerous way to run your music business. Why? Because a creditor (someone that you owe money) may be able to pursue your personal income, property you own, and money in your bank account to repay any debts your business owes them. This exposes you to more risk and potential liability when running your music business.

A sole proprietorship means that you are fully and *personally* responsible for everything your business does. In the law, we call this being held "personally liable" for the actions of your business. For example, if you break a contract with a local restaurant by not performing on the date that you agreed to perform, the restaurant may be able to sue you *personally* for their loss. This means that instead of your company being responsible for the loss and paying it out of your business checking account, the restaurant could possibly get a judgment, or court order, against you *personally* that may allow them to seize (take) assets or property that you own personally (money out of your personal bank account or money from your paycheck) to satisfy (pay back) the amount you owe them.

Example: Marcus is a recording artist. He took a trip with some friends and completely forgot that he was booked to perform as the featured artist at a popular nightclub for their major summer concert. When Marcus came home from his trip, he was served with papers to appear in court personally. The nightclub owner had hired a lawyer and sued him *personally* for the money they had to refund for tickets to the concert. They also sued him for the money they had to pay their attorney to file the lawsuit, court costs and interest. The nightclub received a judgment in their favor giving them the legal right to remove some of the money Marcus owed them from his personal bank account. The rest of the money Marcus owed them would be automatically taken out of his paycheck each week until the balance he owed was fully repaid.

Who wants to live life knowing that at any given moment, someone can sue you for almost everything you personally own and then use the judicial system to take it? Certainly not me. However, this is the risk that you are putting yourself in if you are currently doing music without having formed a business to protect yourself.

You should also know that a sole proprietorship ends when the owner dies. That means that if you ever have plans in the future of selling your music business, a sole proprietorship may not be the best choice for you. This is because many investors are looking to buy a system, or business model, that can continue to make money without relying on one individual. Keep this in mind when you are choosing the type of business you want to form.

Partnerships (General): Twice as Risky!

The next business entity we will discuss is a partnership, which is sometimes called a general partnership. A partnership is very similar to a sole proprietorship – only worse due to the risk. It is similar to a sole proprietorship because you do not have to file any paperwork with the state to set it up. In fact, you do not even have to have a written agreement with your business partner.

Instead, in most states, partnerships start when at least two people agree to share the money they make as well as share any business losses. You can even have unlimited partners. This is the main difference between a partnership and a sole proprietorship. Partnerships can be considered sole proprietorships that require two or more people.

When people think of partnerships in the music industry, they think of a creative collaboration between two talented people. Please understand me. There is nothing wrong with starting a business with a business partner. In fact, it can be very helpful. However, you may want to file the paperwork in your state to form a *limited partnership, corporation, or limited liability company* (discussed below) instead if you want to involve other people in your music business.

The danger of partnerships, like sole proprietorships, is that since you are not formed or incorporated in the state, they do not offer much protection from liability. In fact, they expose you to twice as much risk as sole proprietorships since both partners are responsible for the debts of the other partner. This means that your business partners can enter into contracts and legally commit the partnership and you can be held *personally* responsible for those debts and commitments - even if you did not agree to them.

Example: Cory is a talented performer. Travis is a college student. They agree that Travis will contact restaurants and book performances for Cory. They will split the money 50/50. However, as they start making money, Cory feels he should get more since he is doing more work. They argue. Cory takes their business credit card (which they applied for to advance costs before performances) and bought clothes and expensive studio equipment without telling Travis. He hid the bills for months. He later decided to quit the partnership and left town without telling Travis how to reach him. Travis discovered his credit was damaged and that he was responsible for the payments since they were in a partnership. Travis had to sell his car and work a second job while in school to repay the debt since he was legally responsible as a partner.

Why You Should Register Your Business

There is a better way. Instead of putting your financial future in jeopardy every time you choose to do something with your music business or with a business partner, you can register your business by filing the required paperwork with your state (we will discuss this process later in the chapter). If you decide to register your business, you are taking a step toward separating any legal obligations the business may have from yourself as an individual. This means that if you are paid to produce an album for an artist and the artist wants to sue you because they feel that you did not perform as promised, they likely would not be able to file a lawsuit against you as an individual but would have to sue the business. The business would then be responsible for paying any money owed out of the money available in the business' bank account. Of course, this "limited liability" or protection from being personally liable for the debts of the business, only applies if you also follow very specific rules regarding the way you run your business (which we will discuss later in the book).

Example: Lisa is a producer. Instead of buying studio equipment herself, she rented studio time at her friend's apartment. She used the money she saved to hire a lawyer to form her business "Lisa Sounds, Inc." When one of her clients, a record label, sued her for not completing the production work on an album after she was in a car accident, Lisa was protected. The record label was only able to sue "Lisa Sounds, Inc." instead of Lisa personally because she had formed a business. They also could not touch Lisa's personal bank accounts or paycheck because the law protected her personal assets.

Business partnerships can work. In fact some of the largest and most successful music companies were formed by more than one individual. Therefore, if you want to get other people involved in your business, I generally recommend that you file the paperwork in your state to form one of the entities we are about to discuss. Unlike sole proprietorships and general partnerships, these entities offer "limited liability" or protection from being personally liable for the debts of the business.

Limited Partnership (LP)

The first business entity that we will discuss that offers some liability protection is a limited partnership (LP). A limited partnership is always preferred over a partnership because it allows at least one partner to limit their exposure or risk in the business. Like a partnership, a limited partnership has to have two or more people involved. However, a limited partnership must have at least one "general partner." The general partner is the partner that will be running the business and will be held personally liable for decisions. A limited partnership is also required to have at least one "limited partner." A limited partner is the "silent" partner that does not have any management authority and cannot be actively involved in running the business. However, the limited partner is only liable up to the amount of their capital contribution (the money they initially put into the business).

Example: Angela loves music but enjoys her career in the non-profit industry. She heard Kim perform at a benefit concert in the community and invited Kim to lunch. Over lunch, she asked Kim if she would be interested in the two of them forming a limited partnership. Angela would front the money for Kim to get studio time to record an album, make CDs, and promote the project. In exchange, Angela would only be liable up to the amount she would put in the business ($5,000) but would receive 40% of profits in return for her investment.

As a professional in the music industry, you do not have to do everything yourself. There are people that have capital (resources) but do not have talent and are looking for talented and hardworking people they can invest in. As a result, you can setup a limited partnership. However, unless you are the "limited partner", I always recommend that my clients setup one of the other business entities that we will discuss next because they allow all of the co-owners to have "limited liability" or protection from being held personally liable for the debts of the business.

Limited Liability Company (LLC):

Safe & Flexible

A Limited Liability Company (LLC) is a popular option for structuring your music business for many reasons:

1. **Limited Liability.**

Owners are not liable (responsible) for the debts or claims of the business. Instead, these commitments would have to be paid for from the business assets.

Remember, certain rules have to be followed for the protection to apply. Owners must keep the business separate from their personal assets (discussed later), must act responsibly and cannot engage in illegal and unethical actions.

2. Unlimited Owners.

You only need one owner to start the business. But you can have as many owners as you want. With LLCs, owners are called "members."

3. Informal operations.

1. You do not need a board of directors like a corporation.
2. The LLC can be run by the owners (member managed) or run by a separate manager (manager managed)
3. You do not have to hold meetings or write minutes or notes from the meetings.

I always recommend that you still vote on major decisions (buying or leasing property, major equipment purchases, loans, hiring people) and document them within your business records. You will want to keep copies of these important records in your Corporate Kit (discussed later in this chapter).

4. You are not taxed twice.

LLCs offer pass-through taxation. This simply means that the LLC itself doesn't pay taxes and individual owners only pay once on their tax return.

5. You can still have investors.

Investors are usually owners that are not active in running the business . Be sure to speak with an attorney to make sure you comply with Federal Securities laws if you plan to have people invest in your business that are not working within the business.

6. You have more flexibility with how you divide profits.

You do not have to pay profits based on how much of the company someone owns. Instead, someone can own 50% of the company but you can decide to only give them 10% of profits – perhaps because they are only working in the company and did not invest any money or capital into the business. This is called a "special allocation." You cannot do it just to avoid the amount of taxes someone needs to pay. See an attorney to make sure you are complying with I.R.S. regulations before setting up special allocations.

Example: Jennifer and Christian are brother and sister. They both love music and want to start a business. However, they want something that is easy to run. They setup a LLC. Since Jennifer is putting up the money and Christian is managing their social media accounts, they agree that they will both own the business 50/50 but Christian will only receive 10% of the profits. They hire a lawyer to draw up a contract that lets Jennifer be paid 90% of the profits until she is repaid the full $500 she originally put in the business. After she is reimbursed, they will both receive 50% of the profits.

Profit v. Ownership

Let me take a moment to explain this concept in more detail. The percentage of your ownership interest in a business means that if the business is ever sold, you would receive the same percent of the sale proceeds. If you own 40% of the company and the company is sold for $100,000, you would receive $40,000 from the sale.

Example: Jonathan and Taylor grew their music business over the years. They now have thousands of fans, income from advertising due to website visits and steady monthly income from album and merchandise sales. However, they decide they want to sell the business. Taylor wants to use the money to go back to school and earn his MBA. Jonathan wants to get married and invest his share in buying a house for him and his bride.

They hire a business broker and learn that their business is worth $75,000 (including the value of their studio equipment, copyrights, website, inventory, etc.) Since Jonathan owns 40% of the company, he would receive $30,000 when the company was sold and Taylor would receive $45,000. (75,000 x .40 = $30,000).

LLCs also allow you to receive a different percentage of the profits from the percentage of the business you own if you choose. The percentage of profits you are entitled to receive means how much you will make from current sales or business activities after expenses are paid. If you receive 10% of profits, if the business makes $3,000 from a performance, you would receive $300 ($3,000 x .10)

Example: When they first started the business, they agreed that Jonathan would only receive 25% of the profits since he was designing the t-shirts while Taylor was creating the music, recording it, performing at events, and managing their income-producing website. They made $200 selling merchandise after one of their events. The cost of t-shirts was $125 so their profit was $75 ($200-$125=$75). Since Jonathan receives 25% of profits, he was paid $18.75 ($75 x .25) and Taylor was paid $56.25 ($75 x .75).

Again, make sure you research tax law or speak with an attorney before you setup your LLC with a special allocation (different percentages for profits and ownership). You want to make sure you are in compliance with the I.R.S. so that you do not run into legal trouble in the future.

Corporation: Bring on the Investors

Corporations are another option for structuring your music business. Here are some key factors to keep in mind when considering setting up a corporation:

1. Your liability is limited.

A corporation is separate from its shareholders (owners). If the corporation is sued, the shareholders are only responsible up to the amount they contributed to the business. This is called limited liability. However, in order for the law to continue to treat the corporation separately from the people that own or run it, they must observe corporate formalities (discussed in the next section), act responsibly and not engage in illegal or unethical activity. Otherwise, they can still be held personally liable.

2. You are taxed twice.

C corporations are known for being taxed twice. The corporation pays taxes when it makes a profit. The owners are then taxed on the same funds when they are paid a dividend. Corporations avoid this double tax by paying as many expenses that can be written off as they can during the year. This results in the corporation not having a profit which means it likely would not have to pay taxes.

3. They are structured differently.

Corporations have a (1) board of directors that makes overall policy decisions; (2) officers that run the day to day management of the company; and (3) shareholders or owners that are paid dividends.

Corporations have an advantage over other business entities because they are designed for major growth. Instead of being built to handle a small team of business partners, corporations are designed to support significant numbers of owners and investors. They are able to accommodate complicated profit-sharing structures in order to position a music business for substantial growth. Although other business entities, such as Limited Liability Companies, can also be used to support various investor classes, corporations were intended for this type of model.

Example: Terrence received financial commitments from his father and his mother to give $50,000 toward him starting his own record label. His aunt and uncle also agreed to give $25,000. His goal is to sign several successful local artists to his label, use the funds from his family to promote the artists nationally, and then sell the record label to a major label for a profit of $150,000 after paying back his family.

He realizes he may need even more investor funding to grow the label to a point where it would attract major record label investors. He met with a lawyer that advised him to setup a corporation for his new record label as the best means of achieving his goals.

If you feel that in the future you would like to bring on major investors, multiple business partners and have ownership structures, then a corporation may be the right entity for your music company. Corporations allow you to divide owners and investors into classes. Each class can be given different rights (votes, priority payment of profits, etc.)

Example: Since Terrence would be working full time in the company, his lawyer suggested that Terrence keep 25% equity (ownership) of the business. His aunt and uncle would own 25% for the capital (money) they contributed and his parents would own 50% of the company.

Since Terrence's family does not know much about music or running a music business, his lawyer advised that he structure the company so that Terrence receives Class A stock, which has voting rights in the business. This means that he will have the right to make decisions for the business.

His parents will receive non-voting Class B stock which lets them be repaid the money they invested before any profits are paid since they risked the most. His aunt and uncle will receive Class C stock, which are non-voting shares that are repaid after Class B.

However, since corporations are designed to accommodate large groups of people with different rights, they require a substantial amount of paperwork and documentation. It is not impossible. Primarily, you will need to document or keep a record of decisions made within the business by any of the following groups:

1. Officers
2. Employees
3. Directors
4. Shareholders

5. Company itself

Your state may require you to hold regular meetings, write resolutions documenting major decisions, and provide minutes from your meetings. Also, corporations must follow double-entry bookkeeping procedures since they pay taxes separately from the individuals affiliated with the company. If you prefer a business entity that is easier to manage, then a corporation may not be for you. However, with the help of an accountant and business attorney to advise you, a corporation can still be a good option.

S Corporations

Another way corporations can avoid being taxed twice is to choose to be an S corporation. S corporations protect their owners from personal liability without being taxed twice. They are similar to LLCs and LPs but there are some important differences:

1. You can only have 75 or less shareholders;

2. All shareholders must be U.S. citizens (not businesses).

3. You cannot have more than one class of stock

How to Setup Your Business

Now that we have discussed the various types of businesses and ways you can structure your music empire, let's discuss the specific steps that you would take to setup each one.

How to Start a Sole Proprietorship:

1. **Register your fictitious name in your state.**

If you are using a name for your business other than your legal name, you need to register the name you are using. Search for "Secretary of State of Florida" (insert your State) and they will provide you with the form and filing fee to register a fictitious name.

1. A fictitious name does not provide you with a trademark or legal ownership to the name.

2. You can still be sued for using a fictitious name if someone else already legally owns the name.

3. Conduct a complete search before choosing the name. You do not want to spend money building your brand (website, logo, album artwork, merchandise) only to lose it due to being sued for trademark infringement. We will discuss how to conduct a name search in the chapter on Trademarks.

My **law firm** also conducts name searches for clients all of the time. We examine all federal trademark filings, state trademark filings, company filings in every state, domain names, and common law listings to make sure our clients are not using a name that they will be sued for later.

2. Register to pay Sales Taxes.

Contact the agency within your state to setup an account to collect and pay sales taxes on the goods (albums, etc.) you sell. You should be able to search "sales tax certificate in Florida" (insert your specific state) which will take you to a government website to register.

Make sure you pay this tax on time or you may have to pay late fees and penalties.

3. Get a Business License

You may still need a local, county or state license depending on where you live. Look up "business licenses in Orange County" or your particular county to see if you need one. You can also speak to a business attorney for advice regarding the proper licenses you need in your particular State.

How to Start a General Partnership:

1. Register your fictitious name in your state.

Reference the instructions for filing for fictitious names in the previous section on Sole Proprietorships.

2. Register to pay Sales Taxes.

Contact the agency within your state to setup an account to collect and pay sales taxes on the goods (albums, etc.) you sell. You should be able to search "sales tax certificate in Florida" (insert your State) which will take you to a government website to register. Make sure you pay this tax on time or you may have to pay late fees and penalties.

3. Prepare a Partnership Agreement.

Everyone gets along at the beginning of a partnership. However, once you start making money, people can change. It's important to have the "rules" of how you agree to run your business established up front to avoid disagreements, confusion, or a business partner "making up rules as they go along." Here are just a few of the items you need your partnership agreement to cover:

1. **Your roles.** Will both of you work in the business? What are your roles?

2. **Ownership.** Will you both own equal shares of the business?

3. **Decisions.** Will you both have an equal say when you make decisions? Do you need each other's approval to apply for a loan for the business? Enter a contract? Hire people? What happens if you disagree?

4. **Profits.** How will you split profits? Will you both receive the same percentage of the money you make?

5. **Capital.** Will you both contribute money to the business? Will this money be repaid as a loan or will it remain in the business as seed money?

6. **Death.** What happens if a member dies? Does their share of the business go to their family? Or to the other partner?

7. **New Partners.** Under what circumstances can you add new partners to the partnership? How much do the new partners have to pay to enter the partnership?

8. **Assignability.** Can you assign or give your interest in the business to someone else if you no longer want to be involved? Are you obligated to work with a new partner if your partner assigns his interest to someone you do not want to work with?

9. **Intellectual Property.** Who owns the songs you write? Who owns the name of the business? Who owns the logo?

How to Start a Limited Partnership:

1. **File a Certificate of Limited Partnership in your state.**

Search the internet for "Secretary of State of Florida" (insert your state) and they will provide you with the form and filing fee to register your limited partnership.

2. **Register to pay Sales Taxes.** (Same as Partnerships).

3. **Prepare a Limited Partnership Agreement.** (Same as Partnerships).

How to Start a Limited Liability Company (LLC):

1. **File Articles of Organization in your state.**

The Articles of Organization serve as the formal charter document for your business. They must be prepared based on your state's specific rules. Please view the reference section at the end of this book for a list of state websites in order to file your Articles. You can search the internet for "Division of Corporations in Florida" (insert your state) and the state's business website will provide you with the form and filing fee (amount you need to pay) to file your Articles. A few things to keep in mind:

- Forming a LLC with a specific name does not provide you with a trademark or legal ownership to the name.

- You can still be sued for using a name if someone else already owns the name. You need a federal trademark in order to own your band or artist name. We'll discuss this more in the Chapter on Trademarks.

- Conduct a complete search before choosing the name. You do not want to spend money building your brand (website, logo, album artwork, merchandise) only to lose it for trademark infringement.

My **law firm** conducts these searches for our clients all of the time. We examine all federal trademark filings, state trademark filings, company filings in every state, domain names, and common law listings to make sure our clients are not using a name that they will be sued for later.

2. **Request a Tax ID number from the I.R.S.**

- You can apply for one for free.
- A Tax ID number is like a social security number for your business.
- This allows your business to pay taxes separately from your personal taxes.
- You can search the internet for "tax id number" and you should be able to find a link to the I.R.S. website to apply for a tax ID number.

3. **Register to pay Sales Taxes.** (Same as partnerships above).

4. **Prepare Operating Agreement.**

I always advise that you spend a few hundred dollars and have your Operating Agreement drafted by an attorney that has experience with music businesses and is able to customize your Operating Agreement based on the goals of your music business. This document is very important because it outlines how you will run your business. An Operating Agreement will contain many of the same terms as the Partnership Agreement (discussed above). However, it should also include these clauses, among others:

- Ownership Structure / Membership Classes – LLC owners are called "members." Will there be different classes of members with different voting rights and ownership percentages? Or will there be only one class of members with the same rights and privileges?

- Tax Treatment – Will the LLC be taxed as a partnership or S corporation? For a more complete discussion on business taxes, check out the second book in the Music Law™ series *Run Your Music Business™*

- Distributions – When the company makes a profit, will profits be distributed (paid out) to owners immediately? Or will they be reinvested in the company?

- Management – Will the company be run by the members (owners) or an outside manager?

- Salaries – Will members receive fixed salaries in addition to their profit distributions? If so, how much and how often?

- Liability of Members – Will the Company indemnify (promise to pay the legal fees or costs) of the members if they are sued? If so, under what circumstances?

- Non-competition – Can members also own interests in competing businesses?

- Dissolution – Under what circumstances will the company be dissolved? What is the process for dissolution? Who will be repaid first?

How to Start a C Corporation

1. **File Articles of Incorporation in your state.**

This is the formal charter document for your business and must be prepared based on your state's rules. Again, make sure you conduct a complete search of the name. Please view the reference section at the end of this book for a list of state websites in order to file the Articles for your business. You can also search the internet for "Division of Corporations in Florida" (insert your state) and the state's business website will provide you with the form and filing fee (amount you need to pay) to file your Articles.

2. **Request a Tax ID number from the I.R.S.** (See LLC above)

3. **Register to pay Sales Taxes.** (Same as partnerships above).

4. **Prepare Corporate Bylaws.**

This document should be customized for your music business and should outline how you will run your business.

5. **Issue Company Stock Certificates**

Ownership in a corporation is called stock. You can have custom certificates made to evidence your ownership.

6. **Shareholder Agreement** (Same key terms as partnership agreements above).

How to Start an S Corporation

1. **File Articles of Incorporation in your state.**

This is the formal charter document for your business and must be prepared based on your state's rules. Again, make sure you conduct a complete search of the name. Please view the reference section at the end of this book for a list of state websites in order to file the Articles for your business. You can also search the internet for "Division of Corporations in Florida" (insert your state) and the state's business website will provide you with the form and filing fee (amount you need to pay) to file your Articles.

2. **File Form 2553 with the IRS.**

This is the form you must file for your C Corporation to be viewed by the government as an S corporation. You must file it by the third month or 15th day of your tax year.

3. **Request a Tax ID number from the I.R.S.** (See LLC above)

4. **Register to pay Sales Taxes.** (Same as partnerships above).

5. **Prepare Corporate Bylaws.**

This document should be customized for your music business and should outline how you will run your business. (Same as with Corporation above).

Hiring Someone to Setup Your Business

I have just shared the steps that you can follow to setup your music business yourself. As I shared previously, you can search for the words "Division of Corporations in Florida" (or your specific state) online to find the government website in your state that registers businesses. Their website will show you the exact forms to file as well as the filing fees. You can also view the reference section at the end of this book for a list of state websites in order to file the Articles for your business. This is the least expensive way to setup your music business.

However, if you would like to spend a little more, you can setup your business online using an internet company. You will typically pay around $500 for these services. Please be careful because these companies are not licensed attorneys so they cannot provide you with legal advice or guidance if you are setting up your business incorrectly. Each state has different laws so you will want to make sure that the internet company that is completing your forms is in compliance with your state's most recently passed laws. You'll also want to make sure that the price that is advertised includes everything you need. Some websites will advertise $99 for Incorporation but do not tell you that the price does not include the $125 state filing fee, $75 tax identification number fee or $100 registered agent designation fee.

The last way to form your business is to hire an experienced lawyer to setup your business for you. You can search for "business lawyer in Orlando" (specify your city) online and will see a number of attorneys that are available to help you. My law firm routinely provides this service for clients. Believe it or not, hiring an attorney to setup your business is most likely not as expensive as you may think. In fact, my firm only charges a few hundred dollars more than the internet companies but our service includes everything.

For example, our process begins with an in-office or telephone consultation where we answer our client's questions, recommend the best business type for them based on their goals, analyze the tax implications of their decisions, draft their partnership agreements and share valuable information on how to run their business while remaining in compliance with the law. We then file all of the legal paperwork for them so that they know everything will be structure correctly the first time. Lastly, we remain accessible to them to answer future questions, to draft and review contracts and help them grow.

Regardless of if you decide to file the forms yourself or hire a professional to prepare them for you, the most important thing is to setup a company to protect your business interests.

When Should You Start Your Business?

Clients often ask me "when do they need to invest in forming their business?" I believe in forming your business as soon as you can. It is an investment that pays for itself due to the protection from liability, the professional image that it gives your music company, and the fact that you can deduct business expenses (even legal fees) from your taxes. Of all the clients I have represented, none of them ever expected to be sued. Knowing that your personal life savings are not at risk makes it a more than worthy investment.

However, worst case scenario, I certainly recommend forming it no later than when you begin making money. Meaning, if you are booking gigs, selling your music, writing music with other artists, signing artists to your label, renting studio time, producing or mixing music you plan to sell, writing and making songs available to the public, then you want to make sure you are protected from liability. As a producer, you will want to start a production company. If you are an artist, musician or member of a band, you will want to form a business entity in the name of the band or your artist name so that your band members are not held personally liable. If you are a songwriter, you will want to form a company to sell your songwriting services and perhaps even your own publishing company. If you are an artist that also writes songs or produces, you may want to consider starting your own record label, production company, and/or songwriting company.

Have you ever heard the adage "Don't put all of your eggs in one basket?" Well, the same holds true in the music industry. You will want to setup different companies for each business venture as soon as you can afford to do so. Why? Because if all of your businesses are under the same company, then someone that wants to sue you based on one aspect of your music business (e.g., music production) will have access to your assets from the other business ventures (e.g., songwriting, record label, etc.) if they are all under the same company. As convenient as it may seem to have one "umbrella" company, major record companies and industry professionals always form separate entities to minimize the chances of someone being able to sue them and taking *everything.*

Benefits of a Business Partner:

Another common question that clients ask is "Should they start their music business with a business partner?" Perhaps they are a really talented artist and have a friend that is a gifted music producer. Here are some benefits to starting your music business with a business partner:

1. Your business partner may have knowledge and experience that you do not have that can help you grow your music business.
2. Your business partner may help keep you accountable. Knowing that you have to give a regular update to someone else may help keep you focused on your goals.
3. Your business partner may have industry contacts (promoters, studios, restaurant owners, record label executives, A&R

representatives, media contacts, etc.) that may be helpful to your music business.

4. Your business partner may have skills that can be used for the business (e.g., your partner may be a lawyer, accountant, studio engineer, graphic designer, photographer, musician or vocalist, etc.) without having to wait until you have the money to hire someone with the same skills.

5. Your business partner may have access to resources (money, studio space, office space, and/or equipment) that they allow you to use for the business without you having to purchase these items yourself.

6. Your business partner may provide a more professional image for your business. If you are a new songwriter, producer or artist, it may be helpful to have a business partner that has more industry experience.

7. Your business partner may be able to share the workload of the business to allow you to get things done faster.

8. Your business partner may be able to provide valuable feedback to help you make better decisions.

How to Protect Yourself in a Business Partnership:

1. **Make sure you have similar values.** A successful partnership takes more than both people having something to contribute to the business (e. g., talent, money, time, etc.). You need to agree on your overall business philosophy. Will you pay companies and people you hire promptly? Will you treat your clients and staff with respect and courtesy? Will you be professional and arrive early at

events? Will you keep your business commitments? How important is the business versus family time and other commitments? What type of music are you willing to make? What types of places are you willing to perform?

2. **Make sure you have similar business goals.** Is your goal to create a business you can work in forever or to eventually sell the business for a profit? Is the goal to sign with a major record label or stay independent? Is the goal to make music that you love or make music that sells the most? Is the goal to be mainstream or to faithfully serve a specific market? Is the goal to sign new artists and expand or to simply create a music business that can support you both full-time? How much money is enough?

3. **Make sure everything is in writing.** As previously discussed, you will want to make sure your agreement with your business partner is spelled out in a contract so that your interests are protected.

How to Avoid Being Sued Personally

Now that we understand the various types of business entities that we can form as well as the benefits associated with each one, it is imperative that we also understand how we need to run the business in order to take advantage of the full legal protections it offers. It is not enough to setup a business with liability protection in order to protect yourself from being sued personally. That is like purchasing a car but not knowing how to maintain it to keep it running well.

Even if you have setup your business, you can still be sued personally if the other party (person that is suing you) can "pierce the corporate veil." This is a legal phrase that means you are not running your music company like a separate business but instead running it as an extension of yourself. In order for the limited liability protections to operate, the business needs to be treated like a business – completely separate from you as an individual. This means separate bank accounts and all.

Many songwriters, artists, and producers setup their businesses online without realizing that they need to follow "corporate formalities" in order to show that their business is separate in order to keep their protection. Otherwise, a lawyer can still sue a person with a business personally.

Here are some very important tips to make sure that you run your music business properly in order to remain protected from being held personally liable for the debts of your music business:

1. Don't mix your money.

Establish a separate bank account for the business. Pay yourself in the form of a check instead of making arbitrary cash transfers and withdrawals from your business account. Pay personal expenses from your personal account. Pay company bills from your business account. If owners make loans, write a promissory note with interest and write a check payable to your business. Purchase different color checks to distinguish the two accounts. If someone looks at your online banking statement for your business, they should not see movie ticket purchases, shopping sprees, or other random personal expenses. Instead, all of the transactions should be specifically related to the business. Visit www.IRS.com to learn more about the expenses that qualify as legitimate "business" expenses.

2. **Sign on Behalf of the Business.**

Avoid signing contracts with your individual name. Instead, use a signature block anytime you are signing a contract on behalf of your business:

ABC Company, LLC

By:_____ (Type your name)
Its: Member Manager

3. **Keep Money in the Business Account**

There is no set amount required by law since businesses vary. However, make sure you keep enough funds in the business account to meet current obligations and bills – even before paying yourself. That means if your business bills are $800 each month (including website costs, studio costs, office space, etc.) then you need to make sure you always have at least $800 in the account each month.

4. Put it in Writing.

You should have written contracts for business transactions that plainly state your policies. Make sure these contracts are custom to your business, not just generic forms, so that they will protect you from the unique liabilities associated with your music business and hold up in court. I always recommend having an attorney prepare your initial contracts. You can then continue to use the same contract for a long time.

5. File your Annual Report.

Most states will require that you file an annual return, often referred to as an Annual Report with the state or the Division of Corporations every year to maintain the "active" status. The annual return is due at a specific time each year and penalties for failing to file can be costly (in some states, it can be around $400 and the fee typically cannot be waived). Make sure you file early to avoid these late fees.

6. Pay your Business Taxes.

Make sure you file the proper tax forms and pay your business and personal taxes on time every year. Also, register to pay sales tax if you are engaging in the sale of goods. See a certified tax advisor for more information.

For an in-depth discussion on which specific tax forms you need to file for each business entity, please reference the second book in this series entitled "Run Your Music Business" (www.RunYourMusicBusiness.com) which explains recordkeeping and business taxes for music businesses. You can also visit the I.R.S. website (www.IRS.gov) or speak with your accountant.

7. Keep Good Records.

Keep your receipts, bank statements, returned checks, contracts, invoices, etc. for your records. We recommend that you invest in financial management software to keep track of your transactions.

One of the best ways to keep track of all of your business records and important legal documents is to invest in a Corporate Kit. You can have one made for any type of business (corporation, LLC, partnership, etc.) A Corporate Kit is an elegant, custom-made portfolio with your company name engraved that is specifically designed to keep all of your important corporate and legal documents. You will want to keep your original filed Articles, Partnership or Operating Agreements, Bylaws (if you have them), meeting minutes, resolutions, etc. within this portfolio.

Corporate Kits often include actual corporate seals that you can use to signify that a document is an official document of your business. They also include formal Share Certificates or Membership Certificates with your company name that you can give to your current or future investors or business partners to evidence their investment in the business. Corporate

Kits include ledgers to document how much capital or funds you and/or your business partners invested in the company and track any changes in ownership percentages (if you sell your shares or purchase more). You should of course keep digital or scanned copies of these records as a backup, but a Corporate Kit is an excellent way to keep up with your important originals. Contact our law firm at **http://www.ChisholmFirm.com** for details on ordering a "Corporate Kit" which includes custom stock certificates for your music business.

8. **Document Decisions with Resolutions.**

Document major company actions by writing a resolution on behalf of the company ratifying the decision. Keep resolutions on file in your Corporate Kit.

9. **Choose business names carefully.**

Avoid forming multiple companies whose names are too similar to your other companies. This can create a presumption that all of the companies actually being run as the same company and should be held liable for each other's actions.

10. **Update your Agreements.**

Make sure you update your Partnership Agreement, Operating Agreement, Shareholder Agreement or Corporate Bylaws before you make major changes within your business (e.g., bring on partners, hire people, loan money to the business, transfer ownership, etc.)

Now that we have discussed the different types of businesses, how to set them up, and ways to protect yourself once you have setup your music business, let's discuss how to protect your name with trademarks.

Chapter 2: Protect your Name

THE IMPORTANCE OF YOUR NAME.

In the music industry, the name you choose as an artist, band, producer, or record label is very important. Your name is what fans, promoters, other artists, producers, and corporate sponsors need to be able to remember in order to book you, hire you, and support you. If your name is not catchy enough, or memorable enough, fans and supporters will have a tough time spelling it. Since more and more people look up information on their phones and tablets, if it takes them too long to find you online, they may spend their time locating one of your competitors and supporting their music business instead. Therefore, your goal should be to choose a name that your supporters will remember but also a name that you can legally protect.

How to Legally Protect your Name

Yes, you can legally protect a name. The law provides legal protection for trademarks, which could be the name of your band, record label, songwriting company, or publishing company. By definition, a trademark is a name (words) or a design (logo) intended to distinguish a good or service (your music) from similar goods or services by others in the market (your competition). Therefore, as long as you are using the name of your music business in association with your music services in commerce, you may be able to protect your name as long as certain criteria are met that we will cover in this chapter.

The Difference Between Trademarks & Copyrights

However, before we start our discussion on how to protect the name of your music business, we need to explain the difference between trademarks and copyrights. Generally speaking, you can following these guidelines to understand the difference:

1. Use a copyright to protect your song (music and lyrics)

2. Use a copyright to protect your actual music recording (live performance, studio recording, etc.)

3. Use a copyright to own your album cover artwork

4. Use a trademark to own the name of your band, production company, record label, or artist name

5. Use a trademark to own the logo for your music business

6. Use a trademark to own the slogan or phrase associated with your music business

Why do you need a name you can legally protect?

Now that you understand what a trademark is, we need to discuss how to choose a strong name for your music business that you can legally protect. Why do you need a name you can legally protect? Because you will be investing hundreds and often thousands of dollars in building your brand around this name (e.g. buying a website, logo, merchandise, social media, marketing, etc.) and you want to choose a name that will have maximum legal protection to prevent other people from copying your music company's name and using your good reputation to make a profit. Your name also needs to be a name you can protect and own legally so that someone else does not sue you for using their name and good reputation.

Example: Dane was a songwriter and musician in Michigan. He chose the artist name "Great Dane" for his music business. He searched on Google and did not think it was being used. He paid to setup an LLC, paid for a logo, purchased t-shirts and had a custom website designed with his new artist name. After doing a few shows, he received a letter in the mail from an attorney in New York. The letter demanded that he immediately transfer ownership (user names and passwords) to his social media accounts (Facebook, YouTube, Twitter) with the name Great Dane, his website domain, and immediately stop selling merchandise, making albums, and promoting songs under the name since a country western artist named Great Dane in New York already owned the name. Dane lost the $3,000 that he had invested in building his brand plus all of the potential fans and promoters that knew him under the old artist name.

How do you know if you have a name you can legally protect?

Trademark law is governed by state and federal law. The law provides that you cannot use a name that is similar to someone else's trademark to the point where it may confuse the public and make the public think that you are your competitor. This is called "trademark infringement" or can also be referred to as "unfair competition."

Here are some important factors to keep in mind:

1. You cannot trademark a generic term or something that is commonly used. The United States Patent & Trademark Office (USPTO) will not let you be the only person that can own the rights to a generic term.

2. The name must be used to be protected. If you stop using it and it does not appear that you will start using it again, it may be considered "abandoned."

3. You must use the name in commerce to have rights in the name. You do not receive trademark rights just for coming up with the name.

4. Use in commerce generally means selling or transporting the goods (your music) or displaying the services between states or overseas.

5. You can reserve a name that you have not used, but you still must use it within a certain amount of time to keep your rights.

6. The earlier you start using the name, the better. The law rewards the first user of the mark. The sooner you start using your mark, and preferably register your mark with the federal government, the better.

7. You will only get rights to the mark in the classes (categories of goods and services) that the USPTO deems you are most likely to use or offer to the public. For example, just because you develop rights to your name in association with music entertainment services, does not mean your ownership will extend to pharmaceutical products. Someone else may be able to claim rights to the same name in that particular class if they are using the name in connection with goods or services (e.g., selling pharmaceutical products). You can apply for a trademark in multiple classes (many businesses own a number of trademarks) for additional fees, but

will still have to prove that you actually use your mark within those categories of goods and services.

How do you know if your name is too similar?

Courts will consider several factors to decide if the name you have chosen for your music business is too similar to someone else's name:

1. How similar are the names/marks?

2. How related are their products or services?

3. How strong is your mark itself?

4. In what ways will you market the goods or services associated with your mark?

5. How careful are potential buyers when selecting your goods or services?

6. What was the intent of the infringing person when they chose the mark?

7. Is there evidence that consumers are actually confused between the brands?

8. What is the probability that the companies will expand their offerings to be more similar to the other company's offerings in the future?

How to choose a name you can legally protect

Here are a few factors to consider when choosing a name for your music business:

1. **Easy to spell.** Make sure people will not have trouble spelling your name.

2. **Easy to say.** Make sure the name is not difficult to pronounce. This will make people less inclined to talk about your business since they may be embarrassed about not knowing how to say the name.

3. **Relevant.** It is helpful if your name actually let's people know that your business is related to the music industry instead of a name that makes them think you are in another type of business.

4. **Unique.** The law gives the strongest legal protection to original words that you create yourself (e.g., Twitter, Google, etc.) It is far easier to claim 100% ownership rights to a name that did not exist before you ever used it. You may not want to use your last name because last names are not considered strong marks.

5. **Ask for Feedback.** Feel free to ask close friends or mentors to choose between your top options. However, you may want to consider having them sign a confidentiality or Non-Disclosure

Agreement (NDA) to make sure they do not register and use your name before you do.

6. **Available.** Conduct an extensive name search to make sure that the name is available.

What is a name search?

The only way to know if someone already has the rights to the name that you want to use, is to conduct a professional name search. This involves looking in the most common places where a person could be using the name in order to know if someone already has rights to the name. Here are the places you need to look:

1. **Search for the name online.** Type the name in quotation marks: "Start Your Music Business" to see if any businesses in the same class (offering similar products and services) are using the name or a name very close to yours.

2. **Search Federal Trademark Filings.** Search for the name within the United States Patent & Trademark registrations. Visit **www.USPTO.gov**. You want to look at pending, active, and inactive filings as well.

3. **Search State Trademark Registrations.** All 50 states allow owners to register their trademark on a state level. It is often cheaper than the federal registration process and provides protection throughout

the state – although a federal registration gives you rights throughout all 50 states and can supersede a state registration. You can complete this search by going to the Division of Corporations website for each state and searching their trademark filings for the name you are interested in registering.

4. **Search state company registrations.** All 50 states allow businesses to register their companies. You want to search to see if any other companies are registered using your name. Although registering by itself does not give them rights, using the name with their products and services to the public in commerce does. You can complete this search by going to the Division of Corporations website for each state and searching their corporate filings (be sure to look for all of the business types including LLCs, corporations, etc.) for the name you are interested in.

5. **Search domain names.** You can visit **www.GoDaddy.com** and select the "Who Is" option to see who owns the domain name if it is already taken. Try and search for the company and owner to see if they are actively using the name in association with similar goods and services as yours.

6. **Get a Legal Opinion.** It's always less expensive to do things yourself. However, trademark law is interpreted very specifically. This means that just because *you* feel that your name is not similar,

or *you* feel that someone has abandoned their rights to a name, does not mean the law or a judge would see it the same way. The few hundred dollars that you invest in hiring an attorney to know for sure could save you thousands of dollars defending a lawsuit later down the road.

Our **law firm** conducts a Comprehensive Professional Name Search for our clients. Our name search examines all of the sources we identified above including federal trademark filings, state trademark filings, company filings in every state, domain names, as well as business registries and common law listings. The purpose of this service is to make sure our clients are not using a name that they will be sued for later. We also include a legal opinion where we research any opposition, review the findings and provide you with a legal opinion on the name and if we feel that it is legally protectable based on the law.

How to know if you need a Trademark

Some people think that just because they incorporated or formed their business that they do not need to file for a Federal trademark. However, registering your business does not provide you with legal ownership of the name. Someone else in another state could have registered the exact same name and may have been using the name longer than you have – which would mean they have already acquired ownership rights to the name you are using.

Filing and receiving a fictitious name or "doing business as" (D/B/A) within your state does not give you ownership rights to a name. Some people choose to avoid the investment involved with filing for a Federal trademark by filing for a "fictitious name" instead. However, a fictitious name does not give you ownership or legal rights to the name in and of itself. If someone else was using the name prior to you or had registered a federal trademark, they would have superior rights to the name.

State Trademarks v. Federal Trademarks

Lastly, instead of paying for a Federal trademark, some people apply for a state trademark thinking it will give them the same legal protection. Once again, this is not true. A federal trademark has more weight than a state trademark. Therefore, if you register the name of your music business for a state trademark and someone else registers the same name with the federal government for a federal trademark, their rights would likely be superior to yours. Meaning, they would likely be able to keep the name and you would have to use a different one and possibly be liable to them for damages.

Benefits of a Federal trademark

There are a number of benefits to having a federal trademark to protect the name of your music business. Some of the benefits include:

1. **Ownership.** The first benefit of having a federal trademark is the peace of mind that comes from knowing that you have legal ownership to the mark. This means that if another band or artist in another city, county, or state desires to use your mark, they have to get your permission (unless their use falls within "Fair Use" which is also discussed in this book). This prevents you from spending money buying a domain name, building a website, having a graphic designer create a logo, establishing social media profiles with a name only to have to spend all of the money all over again because you had to take it down since someone else already owned the name.

2. **Make Money through Licensing.** Another benefit of owning a Federal trademark is that it provides another stream of income for your music business. Meaning, once you have built a fan base and have established a brand, you could license, or give other people the right, to use your mark on other products in exchange for paying you a royalty.

Example: Jennifer starts a socially conscious band that builds a substantial following of young adults that love music and appreciate the fact that her band donates a percentage of everything they make to charities. Since all of her fans are familiar with the name of Jennifer's band, and they associate the name with a culture that supports social causes, Jennifer has her attorney draft an agreement with an organic t-shirt company. The organic t-shirt company wants to reach more customers that will be willing to pay a premium for their shirts in exchange for knowing that the t-shirts will not harm the environment. They agreed to pay Jennifer a royalty of 5% for every t-shirt they sell that features her band's logo. This becomes an additional stream of income, or source of revenue, for Jennifer that she does not have to work for. As her group's popularity increases, she strikes similar deals with companies that sell organic coffee mugs, novelty items, work-out clothes, and even a perfume line.

3. **Get Paid when People Wrongfully Use Your Mark.** Owning a federal trademark also means that you have the right to sue someone in federal court for money damages if they use your mark without your permission.

Example: Jennifer finds out that there is a company in Indiana that makes jewelry. They have started using Jennifer's logo (despite the fact that she has a registered federal trademark for the logo) without her permission. The illegal jewelry starts gaining popularity. Jennifer contacts her lawyer and has them send a legal notice to the company demanding that they immediately stop using her legally protected logo. She checks their website frequently and sees that they have not removed the jewelry weeks after having received the notice. She then hires her lawyer to file a lawsuit against the company in federal court. She requests that the judge not only award her the profits that the company has illegally made from selling her jewelry but she also asks the judge to reimburse her for the money that she spent on attorney's fees.

4. **You can get international rights.** Federal trademarks protect your mark within the United States of America. However, if you decide that you want to protect your mark internationally, you can use the rights that you have as the owner of a federal trademark in the U.S. to help build your legal case to apply for trademark rights in other countries.

Example: Now that Jennifer has a registered trademark in the United States for the name of her band, she hears that fans in China have recently discovered her music over the Internet and might also be interested in purchasing merchandise through her band's website. This means that they may also want to purchase items that feature her band's logo that she has licensed to other vendors.

In order to protect her brand from knock-off companies in China that may start selling her products, Jennifer hires her attorney to file to register her trademark in China as well as several other major countries. Since she already has acquired or gained the rights to the mark in the United States of America, she uses this as a basis to apply for rights to the mark in China.

5. **Sell your mark as property.** A Federal trademark is considered intellectual property. This means that oftentimes investors that

may be interested in buying your record label, band, publishing company, songwriting company or production company may want to make sure that you own the rights to your brand before they make an offer. They do not want to risk spending money buying a company only to be sued by someone else later when they begin using the name. Therefore, the mark is something that has value in the market and can be sold.

Example: After five years of touring the world with her band, Jennifer realizes that she is ready to devote herself to the next phase of her life. She wants to focus more on songwriting and advocacy work to promote environmental causes. She decided she would like to start a non-profit and spend the remainder of her career speaking and promoting the values that she believes in.

At first she does not know how she will get the money to start her non-profit. She shares with some of her contacts in the music industry that she is thinking of retiring from her band. Several of her band members, her agent as well as some other record labels express an interest in buying her company including the name and logo from her. She hires her attorney to draft the paperwork and walks away with $70,000 to start her non-profit. She leases office space in an office building, has her lawyer incorporate her non-profit, and begins booking speaking engagements for her new charitable organization.

6. **Use the Symbol.** Owning a Federal trademark also allows you to use the "Circle-R" or "®" registered trademark symbol. This symbol puts everyone on notice that you are the owner of the mark and that they cannot use it without your permission. However, if you use the registered trademark symbol without actually having registered your trademark, you can face Federal penalties.

Common Law Trademark Rights

Believe it or not, you do not have to actually apply for a federal trademark to begin building legal rights in the name or logo of your music business. Generally, the person that uses the name first in "commerce" has the rights to the name as long as no one else used it in commerce before you. Using the mark in commerce gives you "common law" rights to the mark.

However, as we have already discussed, one of the main benefits to registering your name as a federal trademark – instead of just using it and hoping no one else does - is that registering the name makes it much easier to legally prove that you are the actual owner of the name (mark). For example, if you think of a really creative name for your band or group and start using it without registering it, someone else in another state can have their lawyer contact you to sue you to stop you from using their name. If they win in court, you can be responsible for money damages. If you have not registered the name, you will likely have to hire an attorney to try to gather evidence to build a case to prove that you started using the name before the other user did. This can be an expensive and time-consuming process as you may need to hire expert witnesses, prepare testimony and defend yourself in a court proceeding in order to try to prove that you are entitled to legal ownership of the name. If the other side wins, you could end up paying the original owner and lose the ability to use the name for your music business.

On the other hand, if you take the time to register your name up front, you can simply let the person know that you are the registered owner of the name. This statement alone is often enough to discourage someone from challenging your legal ownership of a name.

How to Apply for a Federal Trademark

In order to apply for a federal trademark, you will need to complete the following steps:

1. Visit **www.USPTO.gov**

2. Complete the online Federal trademark application

3. Upload a specimen (sample) of your mark

4. Pay the filing fee (from $225 or $375 depending on which application you choose).

5. Respond *timely* to the inquiries from the USPTO examining attorney until they make a final decision regarding your application.

Completing the Federal Trademark Application

The Federal Trademark Application will require you to provide the following information in order to submit your federal trademark application for consideration:

1. **Ownership Information.** You will need to list the owner(s) of the mark. The owner(s) can be an individual(s) or a business. During the consultation we schedule with our clients of our law firm, we analyze their legal and financial situation to let them know if it would be in their best interest to own the trademarks in their name as an individual, in the name of their business or if we need to form a separate holding company for their trademarks. This all depends on a number of factors such as their individual level of exposure to liability, their long-term and short-term goals for the trademarks, tax implications, etc.

2. **Contact Information.** You will need to provide the USPTO with the primary contact for the application. This information is public record. Most of our clients choose to have our firm listed as the contact so that they do not have

to worry about the examining attorney calling them personally or having their personal contact information made public. Other clients simply want to make sure that all official correspondence comes to us so that they are not responsible for missing a phone call or email and having their application terminated because they failed to timely respond.

3. **Drawing / Depiction of the Mark.** You will have the choice to register your mark as a "standard character" drawing or as a "special form" drawing. Usually, if you are protecting the name of an artist, your company name, or the name of your band, you would use the standard character drawing. This means that the words or numbers themselves would be owned by you. For example, the name "Best Band Ever" would be owned by the band if they use the standard character drawing.

    On the other hand, if they to own their logo or the name of their band written in a special font or design, they would need to file a separate application and choose the "special form" drawing. Special form drawings in particular are governed by very specific rules. I would recommend that you at least speak with a trademark attorney to make sure you are following the guidelines even if you are planning to complete the special form drawing aspect of the application yourself. You should be able to speak to an experienced lawyer for around $150-$400. You can search online for "trademark attorney in Los Angeles" (or insert your city) to find a lawyer in your city. In volume 2 of the Music Law Series, *Run Your Music Business*, I discuss specifically the things you want to look for when hiring an attorney to help you make a wise decision.

4. **Filing Basis.** You will have the choice of stating that you are currently using the mark or that you plan on using it in the future. There are specific regulations regarding the criteria you need to meet for each of these. For example, for the "intent to use" filing basis, you must have the "good faith" intent to actually use the mark. It cannot be something that you plan to register and then never actually use it in commerce. For the "in use" application, you will need to share the actual dates when you first began using the mark in commerce.

5. **Goods/Services.** You will need to show that you are using your mark (or plan to use it, depending on the filing basis that you choose) with actual goods or services "in commerce." This means that if you are filing a trademark application to own your name as an artist, you would need

to list entertainment services as the services associated with your name. Lawyers do this by conducting legal research and evaluating the 45 international classes (categories) that the USPTO uses to classify goods and services. You would then find the class (category) that includes entertainment services and list it in your application along with a description of the specific services that you offer. You can register to own your name in as many "categories" as possible. However, there is a separate application fee of $275 per class (category).

6. **Specimen.** You will also need to include a specimen with your application. The drawing shows the mark itself (e.g., the name "Best Band Ever"). The specimen shows the mark attached to actual goods (e.g., the name "Best Band Ever" printed on a t-shirt if you are applying to own the mark in a class for apparel and merchandise) or services (a business card promoting "Best Band Ever" as being available to perform at concerts, weddings, etc. if you are applying to own the mark in a class for entertainment services).

Can you apply for more than one mark in the same application?

No, you cannot apply for more than one mark in the same application. You can only include one mark (either a name or logo/design) per application. This means that if the name of your band is "Best Band Ever" and your logo is an image of an owl, you would need to file a separate application to own the band name and submit a different application (plus pay a new filing fee) to own the logo.

What is the TEAS Plus application?

Primarily, there are four different application fees based on the type of application you choose. The TEAS Plus application filing fee is $225 per class of goods and/or services in the application. This means that if you want to own your name in multiple international classes (categories), you will need to pay $225 per class (category). For example, if you want to own the name of your band in the entertainment services category as well as the apparel category to protect your merchandise featuring your band's name, your filing fee would be $450 ($225 for the entertainment category plus another $225 for the apparel category).

The TEAS Plus application is less expensive than the TEAS Regular application because you are limited to describing the goods and services that you offer based on the predefined descriptions included within the USPTO's Acceptable Identification of Goods and Services Manual (ID Manual). For example, your band may sell limited edition "henley shirts" in your online store. The ID Manual may not have a predefined description for "Henley shirts" so you may have to simply list that you sell "long sleeved shirts" in general.

In addition, you must meet several other requirements in order to qualify for the discounted TEAS Plus application fee:

1. Your application must be complete when you file it since most of the fields in the TEAS Plus application are considered mandatory.

2. You have to identify the goods and services associated with your mark using the USPTO's Acceptable Identification of Goods and Services Manual (ID Manual).

3. You have to pay for all of the international classes associated with your mark when you file the application.

4. You must file the application as well as any future responses electronically using TEAS.

5. You must consent to e-mail communication and submit a working e-mail address.

What is the TEAS Reduced Fee (RF) Application?

The second type of federal trademark application is the TEAS Reduced Fee (RF Application). The TEAS RF is similar to the TEAS PLUS application but has less requirements:

1. You must file the application as well as any future responses electronically using TEAS.

2. You must consent to e-mail communication and submit a working e-mail address.

In exchange for meeting these two requirements, the filing fee for the TEAS RF application is only $275. It is a little more than the TEAS PLUS application but not as much as the TEAS Regular or the Paper Application.

What is the TEAS Regular application?

The third type of application is the TEAS Regular application. The filing fee for the TEAS Regular application is $325. This application is more expensive because it allows you to describe the goods and services that you offer *without* being limited to the predefined descriptions included within the USPTO's Acceptable Identification of Goods and Services Manual (ID Manual). There are a few more requirements as well:

1. The applicant must include their name and address
2. The applicant must submit a clear drawing of the mark
3. The applicant must list the goods and services associated with the mark
4. The applicant must submit a filing fee for at least one class of goods or services.

Paper Application

The last way that you can file to apply for a federal trademark is by using the paper application. This application has the most expensive application fee, which is $375.

Can you get a refund of your filing fees if your application is rejected?

The electronic trademark application through the USPTO website gives you the opportunity to pay for the filing fee using a major credit card or debit card. However, keep in mind that the filing fees are generally non-refundable. This means that you want to have confidence in your understanding of the process (or the attorney or company you hired) so that you do not have to refile the application multiple times and keep having to pay the filing fee.

How to Respond to the Government's Attorney

Many people mistakenly think that the application process is complete after you submit your trademark application. This could not be farther from the truth! Instead, one of the most important parts of the application process begins *after* you have submitted your application. This is the part where you have to respond to the examining attorney's inquiries.

Approximately three months after you submit your trademark application, the government will assign an examining attorney to your file. This is the trademark attorney responsible for reviewing your application to see if it meets the federal criteria for trademark registration. This attorney does not represent you but represents the government's interests.

The examining attorney will usually contact you with an Office Action. An Office Action is an official letter from the USPTO examining attorney that may ask questions regarding your application, list additional requirements that you need to meet in order for them to consider approving your registration or may include their reasons for denying your application and give you an opportunity to respond.

Either way, once you have filed your trademark application, it is imperative that you reply to the examining attorney by their deadline. The deadline will always be included in the letter and it is usually six months from the date they issue the Office Action. It is your responsibility to keep up with the deadlines and file your responses accordingly. The USPTO will not send you reminders. If you do not respond by the deadline, they may terminate your application and require you to start the entire process over again! This means you also have to repay the filing fees because they are non-refundable.

18 Ways to Overcome a Potential Refusal

Receiving a negative Office Action from the examining attorney is not the end of the world. Here are a few ways you can respond to the examining attorney's Office Action to overcome a potential refusal of your registration. Our firm has successfully used many of these strategies to get our client's trademark applications approved despite seemingly negative Office Actions:

1. Submit arguments against the refusal
2. Attach supporting evidence in support of your argument against the refusal
3. Submit a disclaimer
4. Submit a Stippling statement
5. Submit a Section 2(f) claim
6. Submit a consent to register name(s), likeness(es), signature(s) of individual(s)
7. Make a Supplemental Register amendment
8. Make a Concurrent use claim
9. Submit a new drawing of the mark
10. Submit a better quality image
11. Pay an additional fee for an existing class
12. Submit the $50 fee for losing TEAS Plus status
13. Submit a Signed Declaration to verify an application
14. Modify the identification of goods and/or services
15. Change the filing basis
16. Add/modify dates of use
17. Submit a new or substitute specimen
18. Submit a foreign registration certificate

Again, if the application is not approved, the government will not provide you with a refund. Therefore, you want to make sure that you are confident in your application as well as your Office Action responses in order to give your trademark the best chance at first-time approval.

How long does it take to know if your application is approved?

From the time you submit your application to the USPTO, it typically takes a year for you to find out if your trademark was approved. It can sometimes take longer. However, the important thing to know is that the earlier you file your application the better. Filing early should help give you a head start over any competition that may be considering using the same name. This will allow you to have confidence in knowing that you are investing in a brand that you will legally own and are able to legally protect.

How to Hire Help with the Trademark Process

The federal trademark process can be intimidating and there is a lot at stake. There are several internet companies that advertise low fees to complete the process. However, these companies are not attorneys so they cannot legally advise you on the process. They are limited to allowing you to fill in your own responses. Many of them rely on applicants making mistakes and having their applications denied. Their hope is to have the applicants reapply through them – hence increasing their fees. Not all internet companies are like this – but we have had several clients come to our office after feeling that they were cheated by an online non-lawyer business.

The other alternative is to hire an experienced trademark attorney. For a reasonable fee, an attorney will complete the entire process for you and provide you with the comfort of knowing that it will be filed the right way the first time around. Presently, our firm has a 100% success rate with our trademark filings when the national average is only 41% success (Source: USPTO website). (Disclaimer: Past results do not determine future outcomes). Here is a summary of our trademark process.

1. **Comprehensive name search**. We research and identify any existing threats to our client's ownership of the mark (e.g. name of their band, company, artist, logo, etc.) This includes researching other pending applications as well as any other opposition to the mark. The step is critical because it allows us to let our clients know up front if it will be legally possible for them to own their mark or if someone else already has acquired legal rights to the mark.

If we learn that someone else is already using the mark and has acquired legal rights to the Mark, we let our clients know at the very beginning of the process. We didn't give our clients the option to change the mark that we apply for at no additional cost if their first choice is unavailable. This helps our clients avoid wasting money paying the non-refundable filing fee to the USPTO only to have their application rejected.

2. **Name Analysis.** After we have confirmed that the name is available, we analyze the strength of the mark. This means we evaluate the mark based on the USPTO's criteria in order to know if the application is likely to be approved based on the law. We stay current with the latest trademark laws. If the name does not pass our analysis, we let our clients know ways they can improve the mark in order to increase its chances of approval. Once the mark passes our analysis, we give our clients an official legal opinion with our approval. This gives our clients confidence in the remainder of the application process moving forward since they know that our firm has already legally analyzed the mark and believe that it meets the UPSTO's criteria based on the current federal trademark laws.

3. **Strategic Trademark Consultation.** Once the mark is approved, we schedule a meeting with our client to discuss the various filing options (e.g., character drawing versus special form drawing, black and white versus color design, intent to use versus in use filing basis, supplemental versus principal registry, etc.). We listen to our client's goals and make recommendations so that the registration provides maximum legal protection for them and their brand. We also evaluate all 45 of the international classes before recommending the best classification for our client's trademark. We take into consideration the future of our client's brand in order

to structure a comprehensive plan to protect the mark even as our clients grow and expand into new markets and industries.

4. **Developing Quality Specimen.** We provide digitalization, adjustment and compilation of specimens using our state-of-the-art technology and in-house graphic design department in compliance with the strict USPTO requirements. This prevents our clients from having to file multiple applications with the USPTO and pay additional filing fees due to submissions that do not meet the USPTO's specifications.

5. **Application.** Once we have completed the steps, we file the federal trademark application with the USPTO and provide our client with a copy of the application for their records.

6. **On-going Representation.** We communicate with the USPTO examining attorney throughout the entire application review process by responding to their Office Actions and answering their questions on behalf of our clients. We monitor the application to ensure that deadlines are met so that our clients do not have to worry about their application being terminated due to a missed deadline.

7. **Trademark Certificate.** Once the federal trademark registration is approved, we provide our clients with their official certificate as

well as give them instructions regarding renewing their trademark registrations as needed.

The best news is, our clients are able to deduct 100% of their legal fees on their taxes as a business expense for professional services. Again, if you feel that you may be interested in hiring an attorney to handle the trademark federal application process for you, please be sure to reference the chapter in volume 2 of the Music Law Series, *Run Your Music Business*, where I specifically discuss the things you want to look for when hiring an attorney.

How to protect yourself if someone is using your name?

If you discover that someone else is using the name of your music business, you have several choices.

1. You can ask them to stop. You can send an e-mail or a letter letting them know that you have rights in the name and you are asking that they stop infringing on your trademark and stop using the name.

2. You can ask them to transfer any web accounts that they are currently using with the name to you. You can request that they transfer the user names and passwords to their YouTube, Twitter, Facebook, Instagram, etc. accounts if they are using your protected name.

3. If your request is not successful, you can hire an attorney to send a formal legal notice for you. Our firm has been quite successful with these notices as a means of compelling people to stop using our client's intellectual property and having them transfer the accounts back to our clients. Unfortunately, some people will ignore other people but they rarely ignore lawyers since they know a lawyer can force them into court by filing a lawsuit, which could result in a judgment against them.

How to respond if you receive a notice that you're using someone's name

If you are ever in a situation where you receive a notice that you are using someone else's name, you can take the following steps:

1. Know your rights. Look the company up online to try and find out when they first started using the name. You also want to know if they are using it for similar products and services as you.

2. If you do not feel that you have a case (they have been using it before you started in very similar classes or product/service categories), then you may want to change your name as not to infringe on their rights.

3. If you feel you may have a case, it may be worth hiring an attorney to research the matter to see if they legally own the name. The attorney can also send them a formal response on your behalf

either defending your right to keep using the name or letting them know that you will agree to turn it over to them peacefully.

Now that we understand federal trademarks, the benefits to owning one, how to apply for one and how to protect ourselves if someone ever uses our trademark without our permission, let's learn how to own our music.

Chapter 3: Own Your Music

WHAT IS A COPYRIGHT?

Take a moment and think of your favorite song. There are many ways that a song can be used. The song can be used as background music in a movie or a commercial. The song can be played on the radio and in stores and restaurants. The song can be performed on stage. The song can be performed by a new person with a new musical arrangement. The song can be used as a ring tone for a cell phone. The song can be used as music for a video game.

However, someone has to own the song and have the legal right to make decisions as far as how the song can be used as well as have the right to receive payments when the song is used. That is what a copyright does. The owner of the copyright to a song is the individual, individuals, or business that owns the right to use the song, perform the song, sell the song, make additional copies of the song, make new versions of the song, let other people use the song, and receive payments for the use of the song.

How to Use a Copyright Notice

The simplest way to begin to protect your work is to start listing a Copyright Notice on your work. A Copyright Notice consists of the word "Copyright" followed by the symbol of the letter "C" with a circle around it "©" with the date the song was published and the author's name (e. g., Copyright © 2013, Audrey K. Chisholm). You can use the copyright symbol before you register your song with the U.S. Copyright Office. It is optional to list this on your lyrics and is only required if you wrote your song before 1989. However, I highly recommend that you use the notice. It will help your case if you ever have to sue someone for using your song without your permission. It also discourages others from misusing your song when they realize you have a notice and you are informed regarding your legal rights.

Is Your Music Automatically Protected by the Law?

Whenever you create a song, you automatically own all of the rights to that song as the songwriter or creator. Your musical work is protected by U.S. Copyright laws (The Copyright Act of 1976) as soon as you document it in a tangible or physical way. If you write down the notes or lyrics, email or text them to yourself, or formally record them, you have done enough to give you the protection. However, the difficult part is proving that you wrote it and wrote it first. This is one of the many benefits that registering your work with the United States Copyright Office provides.

Poor Man's Copyright

You may have been told that mailing a copy of your work to yourself and not opening it, known as a "poor man's copyright", provides you with sufficient legal protection to prove that you own your work. However, this kind of protection does not actually exist in copyright law and does not qualify as registering your work with the U.S. Copyright office. Therefore, doing so would not give you the protections and benefits that registering the work with the U.S. Copyright office offers.

Benefits of Registering Your Music

Despite the automatic protection the law gives you as the songwriter, I strongly recommend that you still take the time to file and register your songs with the United States Copyright Office (or hire a lawyer to do it for you) for several reasons:

1. **Registration is Required to Sue** - You have to register as the copyright owner if you want to be able to sue someone in federal court for wrongfully using your music (referred to as "infringing on your copyright").

2. **Reduces Your Fees** – The registration fee is much less if you register your music within 3 months from the date you first

published it or before someone else starts wrongfully using your music.

3. **May Increase Your Recovery** – If your music is registered and you win your lawsuit, you can request statutory damages (which may give you a larger reward) instead of the standard recovery of actual damages you can prove (which are limited to possibly the sales you lost due to the person that wrongfully used your music as well as any profits that person received).

4. **Supports Your Ownership** – Registering as the copyright owner protects you because even if you legitimately wrote the song first, it would be difficult to prove that it was yours alone without a registered copyright. Someone else could then hear you singing or performing the song, register the song under their own name, and begin using the song and making money off of it. You would then have to invest money and time filing a lawsuit against them to try and stop them from using your song and would still have the challenge of somehow proving that you created the song before them.

5. **Receive More Royalties** - You must be the registered owner with the Copyright Office to receive compulsory license royalties (discussed in the chapter on Royalties) from your music.

Therefore, I always recommend that songwriters and musicians take the time to register your songs with the U.S. Copyright Office. You can register your music any time after you create it but the sooner the better.

How to Own Your Music

(Performing Arts Copyright)

When most people think of owning the rights to their songs, they think of the actual lyrics and music that make up the song. The law provides ownership rights for both (1) the lyrics and music as well as the (2) actual recording of the song. The first type of ownership we will discuss involves owning the actual lyrics and music themselves.

A Performing Arts (PA) Copyright protects the actual composition (or song comprised of the lyrics and music). Once you write the song and document it, you are already provided legal protections as the owner of the song as previously discussed. However, I always recommend that you register as the owner of the PA Copyright of the song since it allows you to defend and prove that you are in fact the owner. Typically, the actual songwriter(s) and publishing company (if the songwriter has one) share the ownership of the PA Copyright based on their contractual agreement. However, if you have not signed with a publishing company or have not setup your own, you can simply register as the owner of the entire PA Copyright yourself.

To learn more about starting your own publishing company, get a copy of my second book in this music law series entitled "Run Your Music Business" www.RunYourMusicBusiness.com

Since owning the PA Copyright means you own the composition (music and lyrics), you are entitled to receive mechanical royalties every time a copy of the song is reproduced or distributed. The royalty rate is set by law and is currently 9.1 cents. However, you can negotiate the rate with the record label you have signed with. You can also request that people that want to license (have your permission to use your song) pay you a higher or lower mechanical royalty rate based on your preference. We will discuss mechanical royalties in more detail in the chapter on Royalties.

How to Own Your Music

(Sound Recording Copyright)

The second form of ownership the law provides for songs is the Sound Recording (SR) Copyright. The SR Copyright protects the actual performance itself (e. g., a famous singer's version of a song recorded with her vocals and her band). The owner of the SR Copyright is the owner of the actual studio or live recording of the song. There are certain rights that you receive when you own the sound recording that allow you to prevent other people from making illegal duplications of your actual recording as well as other benefits.

A song can often require multiple SR Copyrights for each of the various recordings of the work whenever new artists record the song. For example, if two popular artists record different versions of a hit Christmas song, they would be able to apply for an SR Copyright for each of the recordings of the song. Of course, they would need permission from the songwriter/publisher that owns the PA Copyright. However, it is perfectly normal for a song to only have one PA Copyright (ownership of the lyrics and music) and many SR Copyrights for each new artist or recorded version of the song.

The SR Copyright owner gets paid artist royalties, also known as master recording royalties. This royalty is typically a percentage of each record sale. The specific amounts are usually worked out between the artist and their record label. However, if the artist recorded the song independently or negotiated to keep full ownership of the recording, then the artist gets to keep all of the master recording royalties themselves.

How to Own Your "Masters"

You may have heard of famous artists sharing how they negotiated that they would own their "masters." By "masters", they are referring to the rights to the master recording or the original recording of the song. They are simply stating that they own the Sound Recording (SR) Copyright to the song as discussed above. In the music industry, the master recording is seen as the final album production of the song. This is the version that all additional copies are made from. As a result, this is the recording that is duplicated and distributed to the public for purchase.

Once you make the recording of the song, you are automatically the owner of your master recording unless you have assigned or given those rights to someone else. However, I always advise that clients register the recording with the U.S. Copyright Office as evidence of their ownership. If you are recording in a studio or working with a producer, you want to have written agreements in place with their signatures showing that you are keeping the rights to your "masters" after the sessions. If you are a producer, you may want to consider having a clause requesting ownership of the master recordings after your sessions.

If you have signed with a record label, you may have a more challenging time keeping the ownership of your master recordings. Typically, many of the agreements that you will be asked to sign as an artist or producer with record labels will require that you give up your right or ownership to your master recordings. It can be very difficult for new artists and producers to negotiate keeping the rights to their masters. Many record labels use the fact that they have resources and an unlimited pool of artists and producers to choose from as leverage to have new talent sign over the rights to their master recordings.

As a result, make sure that you always have an attorney review your record label contracts and that you weigh the costs and the benefits to make sure it is worth it if you decide to give up your rights. Even if the record label is offering you several thousands of dollars up front, those funds may be recoupable, or you may be responsible for paying them back out of the record sales, which means that you could end up like several major artists that sold lots of albums but did not make any money from album sales nor do they own their masters.

How Long Does Your Copyright Last?

If you wrote your song after 1977, your copyright will last your entire life plus 70 years afterward.

How to Protect Your Rights to Album Artwork

You can copyright the cover artwork to your album in the same application as long as you (1) own both the song and artwork (e.g., you designed it yourself or hired someone under contract to give you the rights) and (2) it is being published for the first time.

How to Protect Your Song Title

Copyrights do not protect song titles. If the title is a major part of the lyrics to a song, there may be an argument. Or if the title is unique and has developed a second meaning due to its success and the public identifying it with the work, there may be an unfair competition argument. However, in most cases, your song title will not be protected just by registering as the copyright owner of a song.

How to Register Your Songs with the U.S. Copyright Office

You can register your music with the U.S. Copyright Office by (1) mailing a completed hard copy application to their office or by (2) visiting the U.S. States Copyright Office website and completing their online forms. I always recommend that you register your songs using the online application since your registration is considered effective on the day that the U.S. Copyright Office receives your application. You can also hire a lawyer to handle this for you if you have concerns and want to ensure that it is done correctly. Remember, unless you have an agreement to the contrary, only the creator of a work can register it with the United States Copyright Office.

Here are some simple steps to follow to register your songs:

How to Register Your Songs:

1. Visit **www.copyright.gov**

2. Complete the application.

1. Select "Work of the Performing Arts Copyright" under "Type of Work" for a PA Copyright (Or mail Form PA)

2. Select "Sound Recording" for a SR Copyright (Or mail Form SR)

3. Pay the filing fee. Only $35 for online basic claims

4. Submit a copy of your work.

5. If the mp3 or song file includes both the musical arrangement and lyrics, you do not have to submit the actual sheet music or print out of the lyrics. You can also mail in a hard copy of your work

6. The U.S. Copyright Office will provide you with a certificate as proof of your registration.

Should Your Register Your Songs Individually or as a Collection?

You have the option of registering your entire catalog of songs as a collection by filing just one application with the U.S. Copyright Office as long as you wrote all of the songs yourself (the same person wrote them all). If the songs have multiple writers, each song has to have the same co-writer included in all of the songs for them to be filed in the same application. You should still list the titles of each individual song.

However, know that there is an advantage to registering each of your songs individually instead of registering all of them together as one collection. If someone uses your song without your permission, you can sue them for infringing (violating) 100% of your copyright if you registered the song individually. However, if you registered your songs as a collection, you can only claim that the person infringed on 10% or whatever the percentage that song is out of the collection. Thus, you would have a stronger claim that more of your rights have been violated, which could lead to a larger settlement, if you register your songs individually.

Overall, making the reasonable investment to register your music with the U.S. Copyright Office is a great way to own your music completely and earn maximum royalty income. It also allows you to avoid future legal problems down the road. Now that we understand how to own your music through copyrights, let's discuss how to use other people's music legally through sampling and other means.

Chapter 4: Using Other People's Music

Is Sampling Legal?

Let's begin by discussing the definition of sampling. In the music industry, sampling is using a part of someone else's song, lyrics or music within your own music. In general, if you want to use someone else's music, you have to get their permission. If you sample or use a portion of someone else's music without their permission you are violating United States Copyright law. Therefore, to save yourself the time and expense of being sued, you want to make it a practice of getting permission before you use samples of other people's music or simply chose not to use them at all.

Do you need permission to sample if you are giving the music away for free or accepting donations?

Even if you are giving the music away for free or simply accepting donations, you still have to clear a sample (get the owner's permission) before using it. The song still belongs to the owner and you are receiving a benefit from their efforts, even if it is simply gaining exposure or promotion for your music.

What happens if you do not clear your samples?

If the owners become aware of it, you may be sued for copyright infringement. This means the owners can ask a judge for money damages that you would have to pay. If you do not have a business, the judgment would be against you personally and they could attempt to collect the funds from your personal bank account, savings, paycheck or any property or assets you own. They could request an injunction, which would be a court order prohibiting you from selling or making available any additional copies of the sampled work. You may also have to destroy any other copies in your possession and potentially pay their attorney's fees, court costs, and interest.

When can you sample without getting permission?

Generally, you may not have to ask for permission to use a sample if you are:

1. Not making the music available to the public.

2. You are using the sample at a live performance and the location has already paid fees to license music through performing rights organizations such as ASCAP or BMI.

3. Using the sample in a way that meets the requirements for the "fair use doctrine."

4. Changing the sample so that it could not be recognized by an average user.

What is the Fair Use Doctrine?

The fair use doctrine is an exception that generally says that if you did not use a lot of the original song, if you changed it, or did not cause the owner to lose money in some way, then you can use the song for the purpose of critiquing it, making a parody or using it in a classroom for educational purposes.

However, I never recommend that you sample music based on this doctrine for a number of reasons. First, some courts do not recognize the doctrine depending on the circumstances. Other courts still require a license to be obtained if you are using a sample under the fair use doctrine. Lastly, you would still be responsible for the time and expense of hiring an attorney to defend yourself if you were ever sued when using sample under the doctrine. Therefore, the risks generally outweigh the benefit. To learn more about the fair use doctrine, please visit the U.S. Copyright Office website: www.Copyright.gov

How much can you sample without breaking the law?

Legally, there is no set formula that determines if a song illegally copied another song which is called copyright infringement. Instead, the legal standard to know if a song infringes on someone's copyright is if the songs are "substantially similar." Courts will determine this on a case by case basis. They will listen to both songs to determine how similar they truly are. They can also evaluate evidence (testimony of band members, studio engineers, people you spoke to while writing the song) to know if the first song was influenced by the other song. Courts will consider how significant the portion of the song was that was used by the other songwriter - not just how much of the song was used. Lawsuits are time consuming and expensive so it is easier to be careful to avoid running into trouble from the beginning when you're writing your music. If you find yourself in a situation, make sure that you contact a lawyer as soon as you can to find out your rights.

Despite the risks, some artists and producers still sample music and make their music available to the public. They rely on the fact that (1) they only plan to sell (or give away) a few copies; (2) believe they made the sample unrecognizable; and (3) conclude the owners will never find out. Again, I do not recommend this course of action. There are many songs that were written in obscurity, went viral on the internet, and became hits. The internet and social media have made the world very small and have made it much easier for copyright owners to be notified when their work is being used. Also, making a sample unrecognizable is subjective (based on an individual's own interpretation) and the owners could still argue that their rights were infringed. In conclusion, illegally sampling someone's music is likely not worth risking your music career since there are ways to legally get permission to make sure you are in compliance with the law.

How to Clear a Sample

In order to clear (or get permission) to use a sample, you will need to contact the owners of the song. However, a song may have multiple copyright owners as we previously discussed. Therefore, knowing which owners you need permission from depends on which parts of the song you have sampled in your song. For example, if you sampled the actual recording (e. g., a clip from the song itself as recorded on the album), you will typically need permission, known as clearance, from the person that owns the copyright to the sound recording (the actual recording), which is usually the record label as well as the owners of the composition (PA Copyright). Please reference the previous chapter on copyrights to learn more about SR Copyrights and SR Copyrights.

However, if you simply used the music (similar chords or beats) or incorporated the words or lyrics, you will only need permission from the owners of the PA Copyright, which is typically the songwriter and publisher.

How to Find the Owner of the Composition

Once you have determined that you need permission from the owner of the composition (PA Copyright), you will need to find their contact information. The easiest way to find the owners of the PA Copyright is to look up the song through the major performing rights societies (BMI or ASCAP) that handle licensing and contact the songwriter/publisher to request permission to license or sample their song.

How to Find the Owner of the Master Recording

In order to find the owners of the master recording (SR Copyright), you can search online or look at the album itself to identify the record label that owns the rights to the master recording. Once you have found the songwriter/publisher of the song, you can sometimes contact them to help you find the owners of the SR Copyright. Lastly, you can also hire a sampling consultant, or a company that specializes in finding owners to help you with the process.

What does it take to be given permission?

Most owners will want to hear how you are sampling the music. You can then negotiate a price for a license to use the sample and sign a licensing agreement. A licensing agreement is generally a contract that the owner of the song will sign that gives you the right to use the song. The contract will outline the extent that the owner is willing to let you use the song. For example, the owner may say you can use it for a limited period of time. This is called a non-exclusive agreement since you are only granted permission to use it for a specific time period and they reserve the right to let others use it as well. Or, the owner may give you the exclusive rights to use the song. This means that for the fee you agree to pay, you will be the only person that can use the song.

How much will it cost to clear a sample?

You can agree to pay the owner a flat up-front fee to use the song or they may ask for royalties based on how many copies you make or a percentage of the income the song earns. However, most music songwriters/publishers and owners of the master recording (typically the record label) will each want (1) an advance payment and (2) a royalty from each song sold. Flat fees can range from a few hundred dollars to several thousands of dollars depending on the popularity of the song.

What should you negotiate?

1. Can you use the sample in live performances?

2. Can you use the sample in remixes or other versions?

3. How will you give credit to their work? (e.g., album, marketing, etc.)

Again, please be sure you have everything in writing. I also recommend having an attorney review your contract or prepare your licensing agreement to make sure your legal rights are protected.

What if you cannot find the owners?

I never recommend taking the risk of using a sample without having the owner's permission. Instead, if you are able to find the publisher (which is usually easier to do since they are often registered with performing rights societies and can be easily identified) you can always re-record the song yourself with the publisher's permission. Since you are not using the original recording, you would not need permission from the owner of the master recording (SR Copyright). This would also likely reduce your licensing expenses since you are not negotiating with the PA Copyright and SR Copyright owners but simply the PA Copyright owners.

Here are some other strategies you can try if you are having difficulty locating the owners to clear a sample:

1. **Hire a Consultant.** There are companies that specialize in locating owners and clearing samples. Since they work in the industry, they have contacts and systems in place to speed up the process and do it efficiently. Therefore, you can hire them to find and clear the sample for you. Fees vary but they typically charge $300-$400 per clearance for their services. Here is an example of a company that handles clearances: www.dmgclearances.com

2. **Offer more money up front.** Sometimes making your offer more attractive will convince owners to allow you to use a sample if you absolutely cannot finish your song without it.

3. **Use a different sample.** You can always replace the sample with another sample that has owners that are willing to give you permission.

4. **Purchase royalty free samples.** If you are unable to find the publisher or they do not give you permission, you can purchase samples online that do not require clearance and give you full ownership of the song. Here are a few sites:

   - http://www.royaltyfreemusic.com
   - http://www.royaltyfreemusiclibrary.com/
   - www.stockmusicsite.com

5. **Use a song in the public domain.** You can also try to find a popular song that is in the "public domain". This is a song that you do not have to license, ask permission or pay royalties to use since their copyright has already expired. This generally applies to songs first published in 1922 or earlier. You can find these songs by searching online for "public domain songs."

However, make sure you confirm the copyright date and information first before using it as you would still be legally responsible if you were mistaken and the song was not in fact in the public domain.

How to "Cover" a Song?

When you "cover" a song, you are recording your own rendition of someone else's song. Posting a cover of a popular song can often be a great way to gain exposure as a new artist or producer. Many fans of the established artist will search for the song on the internet or on YouTube. They will find your version of the song and it will introduce you and your talents to a new audience. Since the popular artist is more established, you may receive a lot more traffic and visitors finding your music from "covering" a popular song than you would just posting your own song. A well-done cover can also show your existing fans just how versatile and talented you are as a musician, producer or artist.

Do you need permission to cover a song?

Yes. You will need a mechanical license to record someone else's song and make it available to the public – even if you are giving it away for free or accepting donations.

How do licenses for covers work?

The United States Copyright Act, Section 115, permits anyone to record a song that has already been released to the general public by an artist (even without the copyright owner's permission) as long as they get a compulsory mechanical license and pay the statutory rate for royalties. However, there are some limitations to mechanical licenses:

1. You cannot change the lyrics

2. You cannot change the melody

3. You cannot change the "fundamental character of the song" without the copyright owner's approval.

How to Get a Compulsory Mechanical License

There are several ways to secure a compulsory mechanical license to use someone else's song.

1. **Do It Yourself.** You can get a compulsory mechanical license by providing a Notice of Intent to Obtain a Compulsory License to the owner of the copyright and following the rules enumerated in Section 115. You will also need to provide monthly royalty statements and strictly comply with the requirements of the statute.

2. **Hire an attorney or professional.** You can hire an attorney or professional to clear covers for you.

3. **Use an online company.** There are several online companies that specialize in mechanical licenses for covers. Here are a few:

   - Limelight **www.songclearance.com**
   - Easy Song Licensing **www.easysonglicensing.com**
   - Harry Fox Agency **http://www.harryfox.com**

If you simply need to license music for corporate communications, live events, media programming, and advertising, consider visiting: www.greenlightmusic.com

You can also negotiate directly with the copyright owner to avoid the requirements of a statutory compulsory license by finding the owner using the steps outlined above and making your offer. Record labels rarely use compulsory licensing because they do not want to provide monthly royalty statements or comply with the other strict requirements of the statute. Instead, they contact the copyright owner directly and request a license which allows them to negotiate the terms more freely.

What about Covers on YouTube?

If someone covers a song and posts it on YouTube without clearing the song, the copyright owners can file a lawsuit against them or submit their claim to YouTube. You can also use the same process if you learn that someone is illegally using your music online without your permission. Here is the link to file a YouTube complaint:

http://www.youtube.com/yt/copyright/copyright-complaint.html

YouTube also allows copyright owners to choose to work with YouTube and earn income when their songs are posted on the site. Visit their website for more information.

What if you want to change the song?

If you change the song, your remix is considered by the law as a "derivative work" which requires the copyright owner's permission.

Now that you understand how to use other people's music legally, let's discuss how to protect your legal rights when you co-write a song with someone else.

Chapter 5:

Protect Your Rights when
You Co-Write A Song

YOUR RIGHTS AS A CO-WRITER OF A SONG

I f you have written a song with another person, both of you are owners of the song.

1. One personal does not own the music while the other person owns the lyrics. Instead, you both own a percentage of the total song based on your agreement with the co-owner (e.g., 50/50). If not initial agreement was reached, courts will presume you each own 50% of the song.

2. You can still give other people permission to use the song, which is called a license. However, you would have to share the income from any licensing arrangements with the other co-owner.

3. If you want to sell the song to someone, both of you have to agree to sell the rights as co-owners.

4. You both have the right to file a lawsuit against a person that uses the song without your permission. However, since you both own the song, you would have to share the proceeds of the lawsuit with the other co-owner.

How to Protect Your Rights

As tempting as it may be to just start writing, make sure that you have a discussion up front with the other songwriters, artists and musicians before you begin writing a song with them. For example, if you decide to co-write a song with other artists, make sure that you have both agreed on who will receive the writer's credit. The writer's credit is the person that will be acknowledged for writing the song on the album.

You then want to decide who will receive compensation as the songwriter for purposes of royalties. This is something that should be agreed in advance and you should have a written contract for both songwriters to sign. Having a written agreement in advance may help avoid confusion or lawsuits in the future and will help protect your legal rights in the song.

Example: Dustin and Mark are best friends. They write a song together and Dustin agrees that Mark can have the writer's credit and they will split the ownership and receive 50% royalties each. The song becomes popular online and a major artist reaches out and wants to license the song. Dustin now wants to be listed as a writer on this popular artist's album. He lies and says that he never agreed to let Mark have the songwriter's credit. They end up in court arguing and Dustin wins since Mark did not have any real evidence to prove that Dustin ever agreed to let him have the writer's credit.

It is far less expensive to spend a few hundred dollars having an agreement drafted that you can use over and over than to have to pay several thousands of dollars later in court to resolve a dispute. Therefore, make sure that you have an agreement in writing that spells out who will get credit for the song and the percentage of royalties that everyone involved will receive. If there is ever a disagreement in the future, you can always use the contract in court to defend your legal right to be paid royalties from the song.

What are Split Sheets?

When you are writing or working on music with other songwriters, you need a Publishing Split Sheet. A Split Sheet outlines the credit and royalties each contributor will receive. A properly completed Split Sheet will help to prove your ownership interest in the song. You should still register the song with the U.S. Copyright Office (discussed earlier) but Split Sheets are absolutely necessary when you are writing with other people. According to copyright law, a court can determine that all parties deserve equal ownership even if the other person only contributed one line if there is no agreement that says otherwise.

How to Create Split Sheets

You should complete a Split Sheet **before** you start writing or recording with other people to avoid disagreements later. You will need to complete a separate Split Sheet for **each** individual song you work on. A Split Sheet should include:

1. Writer's Names

2. Writer's Addresses

3. Writer's Performing Rights Organization

4. Writer's Title (Artist, Producer, Songwriter)

5. Writer's Percentage of Ownership in the Song

6. Writer's Publishing Company (if they have one)

7. Writer's Signature, Date, Birthdate

How to Divide Income between Co-writers

There is no set rule to determine how much ownership a contributor should receive. Ideally, the split should be based on how much they contribute to the song. However, you do not have to split the money you make from the song down the middle. Instead, you can decide the percentage or share each co-writer will earn based on how much of the song they wrote. The amount a co-writer is entitled to earn from a song is called the writer's share. Therefore, the more talented writer could receive 80% of the earnings from the song and the other writer that simply wrote a verse could receive 20%. The person that writes the lyrics or music will typically receive more than someone that only contributes a verse. A producer may want as much as 50% of the song. But remember, everything is negotiable and your job is to get as much ownership of the song as you can fairly receive based on your contributions.

You also want to agree on who receives the songwriter credit on the actual album. Typically, this goes to the person that wrote the actual lyrics and primary chords to the song. Special instrumentals often do not typically receive credit as a songwriter.

However, keep in mind that even if you are not listed on the album as a songwriter, you can still be entitled to receive a share of the royalty income from the song if you are listed as a co-owner of the song as a songwriter on the PA Copyright. This will allow you to be listed as a songwriter when you register the song with a performing rights society (ASCAP, BMI, etc.) to collect royalties for publishing purposes.

Now that you understand how to protect your legal rights when you co-write a song with someone else, let's discuss royalties and how you can earn maximum income from your songs and music.

Chapter 6:

Earn Royalties from Your Music

Whenever you write a song, you are entitled to receive royalties or a percentage of the money that the song earns for the life of your ownership of the copyright. You can consider the songs that you write as workers that you will release into the world. These workers will be hired (or licensed) by artists, record labels and producers and will return to you with a paycheck from their efforts (placements on albums) in the market (music industry).

I always advise my clients to try their best to keep as much of their ownership interest in the songs they write as possible. Record labels and publishers will often ask you to assign (give) your rights to them. However, if you have a song with great potential – it may not be worth it. You can lose the ability to have regular streams of income from your song royalties for the rest of your life if you give these rights away.

Royalty income is like having an investment or annuity that pays you an amount each month without you having to work for it. Most investors start businesses or buy shares of ownership in companies in hopes of having an investment that will pay them regularly without them having to work for it. If you build your song catalog strategically by writing popular songs and developing a plan to license them, you can have monthly passive income (money you make without actively working for it).

Good investments can be hard to find. If your gift is writing songs, believe in your future "investment" enough not to sign away the rights to your future retirement fund (your songs) before you have at least given them a chance to work for you and generate a profit.

Now, let's the discuss the different types of royalties that your songs can earn for you:

How to Earn Royalties from Record Sales (Mechanical Royalties)

The first type of royalty that you can earn from your songs is the royalty you earn each time the song is manufactured, reproduced or distributed to the public. Anytime someone manufactures, reproduces or distributes a song written by someone else, they must pay a "mechanical royalty" to the owner of the Performing Arts (PA) Copyright, generally the songwriter and publisher.

Think of a mechanical royalty as the price you would pay the copyright owner for mechanically reproducing their song and making it available to the public (for purchase or otherwise). The mechanical royalty rate is set by the government. Currently, you will earn 9.1 cents per physical recording (CD) and permanent digital download for songs that are 5 minutes or less. If the song is longer than 5 minutes, you earn $1.75 per minute over the initial 5 minutes. Or you can negotiate your own mechanical royalty rate with the person that wants to license your music based on payment terms that you are comfortable with.

How to Earn Master Recording Royalties

Songwriters are not the only ones that get paid every time a song is sold or made available to the public. As a featured artist, you can earn an "artist mechanical royalty" also known as an "artist royalty" or "master recording royalty" every time your song or album is sold. In your record label agreement, be sure to negotiate this and try to get the highest royalty percentage you can since this royalty is negotiable.

If you are an independent artist without a record label, or if you own your own record label, you will keep the entire artist royalty as long as you are the registered owner of the Sound Recording (SR) Copyright, also referred to as the master recording. The SR Copyright gives you the rights to the recording of the song. Therefore, you do not have to worry about paying yourself a royalty since you get to keep the entire pie (the money made from each album or song sold) after paying the mechanical royalty to the songwriter and publisher and recovering your costs (which include the producer royalty and other costs you paid to produce the album). The artist royalty is typically a percentage of the "suggested retail list price" of records sold, which generally ranges from 8% -15%. If you are also the songwriter and acting as your own publisher, then you will keep both the mechanical and artist royalties from the song.

However, if you choose to sign with a record label, you likely will not receive the entire artist royalty. Instead, your record label may offer you an advance, or an amount of cash up front before the album is released. This amount can be offered to you as a signing bonus, for wardrobe expenses, etc. However, the important question to ask your record label before receiving any advances or payments is: "Will this be recoupable?" Meaning, "Do I have to pay this money back?" Many record labels expect to recoup, or have you reimburse or repay, the advances they paid you up front out of your artist royalty generated from your album sales.

Record labels also typically agree to pay for your recording costs, marketing and album promotion. However, you want to ask if these expenses are "recoupable" meaning will they expect you to pay them back out of your royalties? Otherwise, instead of you earning a cut from each record that is sold, the money you earn would go toward paying back the $5,000, $10,000 or even $25,000 advance your record label gave you or repaying the $8,000 they spent for recording costs. Once the "recoupable" expenses are repaid to the label, you would begin receiving your actual artist royalty. However, many artists' albums never sell enough records to fully repay the label and they end of making multiple records without receiving any artist royalties from the album sales.

Alternatively, you can decide to be paid a flat amount per album you record instead of an artist royalty on albums sold and give up your right to an artist royalty altogether. You can also negotiate this rate to decrease or increase it based on your popularity as an artist. Many recording artist agreements pay the producers royalty (discussed below), as well as a percentage for costs relating to packaging, giveaways, and reserves for returns out of the artists' royalty. Even then, the artist receives their royalty payments after the record label has been reimbursed or recoups their costs for recording and often promoting the album.

You can avoid the pitfalls of forfeiting your artist royalty by refusing to accept large "recoupable" advances. You should also make sure that if your record label will be "recouping" the recording costs and expenses for your album, you are at least able to approve the final album budget so that you know exactly how much you will be responsible for repaying.

How to Earn Producer Royalties

Yes, producers can also receive a royalty. Producers can also negotiate to be paid a royalty every time a song or album they produced is sold (usually 3%). Again, this should be included in your producer agreement. If you are a producer, the higher the percentage of your producer royalty, the better! If you are an artist or record label, you will likely want the producer to be paid the least amount possible so that you are able to keep more of the revenue. You may even want to simply pay them a flat fee for their services so that you do not have to give up any of your royalty income.

How to Earn Royalties from Performances, Radio and Television (Performance Royalties)

The music industry rewards the individual or individuals that actually write a song. As the composer or songwriter (the person who wrote the song and music) you are also paid royalties through multiple streams of royalty income. The reasoning is to balance the scales since artists typically receive notoriety for a song and are able to make a living from the name recognition associated with performing the song. Therefore, the performance royalty is supposed to compensate the lesser known songwriter that does not receive the benefit of mass name recognition. However, in the event that you are the songwriter and the artist, you will keep even more royalties.

Here is how it works. If you are the songwriter (owner of the Performing Arts Copyright) and the song is properly registered with a performing rights society (ASCAP, BMI, etc.), the song will earn a performance royalty each time the song is performed in public (e.g., played on the radio, used in a television commercial, played as background music in restaurants or stores, played at a lounge, or used as elevator music, etc.) This royalty can range from: Radio $.15 - $.20 cents per play per song; Television $5-$9 per station broadcasting song. You can negotiate your own contract with your own payment terms yourself or you can use your performing rights society to license your music and pay you your royalties.

The performance royalty is split in half and paid to two parties. One half is called the publisher's share and the other half is called the writer's share. In the past, most songwriters were not artists themselves and typically hired a publishing company to give their music exposure within the music industry. Therefore, the royalty was divided between the publisher and the songwriter. However, today, it is common for songwriters to serve as their own publishers and keep 100% of the performance royalty. Or, your record label may require that they receive the publisher's share and allow you to keep the writer's share. All of these factors are negotiable. However, the more of the performance royalty you are able to keep, the more you will be paid.

How to Earn Royalties from Movies and Commercials (Synchronization or "Synch" Royalty)

The music used in movies and commercials plays a huge role in the film or commercial's overall retail success. Therefore, there is a special category of royalties just for synchronizing songs to other types of media such as television, movies, film, commercials, etc. This royalty is called the synchronization or "sync" royalty. Sync royalties are negotiable and range from $2,000 - $30,000 or more for movies. Television commercials often range from $10,000 - $80,000+. The owner(s) of the Performing Arts (PA) Copyright and owner(s) of the Sound Recording (SR) Copyright (rights to the recording of the song) are entitled to receive sync royalties.

Earn Royalties from Print

If there is demand for your song, a company may want your legal permission to print the lyrics and music as sheet music and make it available for purchase. In this case, the songwriter and publisher are again entitled to royalties. Print royalties are usually paid as a percentage of sales (10-20%).

Earn Royalties from Digital Streaming

More and more people are listening to music through digital streaming such as satellite radio (such as SIRIUS XM), internet radio, cable TV music channels and other streaming platforms. More popular websites like Pandora Spotify, and YouTube also provide opportunities for music streaming. You are still entitled to royalty income when your music is used through these venues. The recording artist that is featured on the song and the owner of the Sound Recording Copyright (master recording) receive a mechanical royalty and the songwriter/publisher receives a negotiated performance royalty. These royalties are typically administered through companies such as www.SoundExchange.com or www.TuneCore.com

However, streaming royalties are being criticized because many artists and songwriters feel that they are not being paid the royalties they deserve. Streaming companies, such as Spotify, make money from charging listeners a subscription fee often to eliminate sponsorships and advertisements. In exchange for this nominal monthly fee, sometimes $5 or $10 a month, they allow their listeners access to unlimited catalogs of music. Each time a listener selects a song to listen to using the streaming service, the streaming company pays a (1) master recording royalty (calculated as a percentage of the revenue the streaming company earns); (2) mechanical royalty of $0.005 (less than a penny) and (3) a negotiated performance royalty to the owners of the song which is often divided between the record label, publishing company, featured artist, and songwriters depending on their ownership interests. Non-Interactive Streaming providers, companies that do not allow listeners to choose their songs such as Pandora, only pay a performance royalty to the songwriter/publisher of the song.

Those in favor of streaming companies argue that the lack of royalty income is made up for by the exposure to new fans that will purchase merchandise, concert tickets, and albums. While others feel that it simply is not worth it since the royalty income is substantially less than other forms of music publishing. Legally, there may be legislation emerging in the future to further control the amounts that performers and owners of recordings are paid in royalties from these types of services.

Earn Royalties from Digital Downloads

In the past, music lovers bought cassette tapes and CDs. Now, you can download your favorite singles as a digital download with just the click of a button through services such as iTunes, Amazon MP3 Store, and Google Play. When a customer buys a single for $.99 on iTunes, iTunes typically charges $.30 from the sale. $.609 is paid to the owner of the master recording (SR Copyright) as a master recording royalty. This is usually either the record label or the artist if they recorded the song independently or were able to negotiate keeping the rights to the masters from their record label. The remaining $.091 is paid as a digital download mechanical royalty to the songwriter and publisher (sometimes the same person) of the song.

Congratulations! You have now completed "Start Your Music Business." Hopefully, you now have a better understanding of how to structure and setup your company, how to copyright and own your music, how to protect your name and logo with federal trademarks, how to legally use other people's music, how to protect your rights when you co-write songs, and how to earn royalties from your music.

However, there is more to know! If you enjoyed this book, I hope you will consider purchasing the second book in my music law series entitled *"Run Your Music Business."* This book picks up where we left off and will explain the following:

1. How to Get Paid Licensing Your Music
2. How to Set-up Your Own Publishing Company
3. How to Build Your Own Music Catalog
4. How to Register with a Performing Rights Society
5. How to Negotiate Contracts (Record Label Agreements, Producer Contracts, Songwriter Contracts, etc.)
6. How to Work Full Time in Music
7. How to Know if Your Business is Growing
8. How to Know if Your Business Is Profitable (Understanding Financial Statements)
9. How to Create a Budget for your Music Business
10. How to Manage Debt
11. 10 Ways to Improve Your Credit Score

12. How to Run Your Music Business

13. How to Hold Business Meetings

14. Developing a Strategic Plan for Your Business

15. Business Recordkeeping / How to Keep Proper Business Records

16. 10 Ways to Avoid I.R.S. Trouble

17. How to File Business Taxes

18. Building Your Team

19. And more!

Visit **www.RunYourMusicBusiness.com** for more information.

Final Words from the Author

If you enjoyed this book, please consider:

1. Leave a review. This helps the book gain more visibility online to help other people.

2. Buy the second book in my Music Law Series™ entitled "Run Your Music Business™" (www.RunYourMusicBusiness.com)

3. Tell a friend (You can also recommend and add the book to your Amazon.com Wish List which helps us reach more people).

4. E-mail me your feedback or questions (Audrey@StartYourMusicBusiness.com)

5. Visit our website for free legal tips, and more! (**www.StartYourMusicBusiness.com**)

6. Follow me on Twitter for free legal tips, special promotions and more. Over 13,000 followers and counting! (@AttorneyAudrey)

7. Like our Facebook page for free legal tips and updates that may not have made it into the book (**Facebook.com/ChisholmLawFirm**)

8. Book me to speak at your next music conference, seminar, workshop, concert or event (**www.AudreyChisholm.com**)

About the Author

Audrey K. Chisholm, Esq. is the founder and senior partner of Chisholm Law Firm, LLC. She is a nationally renowned attorney and represents individuals in the music business in entertainment, corporate, litigation, and intellectual property (copyright and trademark) legal matters. She is a member of the Florida Bar Association. Her clients include Fortune 500 companies, record labels, songwriters, music publishers, producers and artists whose works have been featured on MTV®, American Idol®, VH1® and more. She is a sought after speaker at conferences and events and has spoken to audiences of over 13,000 people. She is the bestselling author of *"Start Your Music Business*™*"* and *"Run Your Music Business*™*"*.

Attorney Chisholm is also the founder of a federally recognized 501(c)(3) tax-exempt non-profit organization, Revolution Leadership®, Inc., that provides educational leadership programming, financial management, and entrepreneurship training, and awards college scholarships to high school students and has served thousands of students nationwide. She resides in Orlando, Florida with her husband, financial author Dr. Juan Chisholm.

For more information, or booking, please visit:

www.AudreyChisholm.com

Twitter: @AttorneyAudrey

Facebook.com/ChisholmLawFirm

For more books and services, please visit:

www.StartYourMusicBusiness.com

www.ChisholmFirm.com

www.RunYourMusicBusiness.com

www.PurposeProperties.org

www.RevolutionLeadership.org

Reference: State Filing Fees for Forming a Business

State	Filing Fee for Corporation	Filing Fee for LLC
Alabama	$160	$160

http://www.sos.state.al.us/BusinessServices/Default.aspx

Alaska	$250	$250

http://commerce.state.ak.us/dnn/cbpl/corporations.aspx

Arizona	$210	$200

http://www.azcc.gov/divisions/corporations/

Arkansas	$50	$50

http://www.sos.arkansas.gov/BCS/Pages/default.aspx

California	$125	$90

http://www.sos.ca.gov/business-programs/

Colorado	$50	$50

http://www.sos.state.co.us/pubs/business/businessHome.html

Connecticut	$250	$120

http://www.concord-sots.ct.gov/CONCORD/

Delaware	$89	$90

http://corp.delaware.gov/

District of Columbia $220 $220

http://dcra.dc.gov/book/about-business-licensing/corporations-division-
corporate-status

Florida $70 $125

http://www.sunbiz.org/

Georgia $100 $100

http://sos.ga.gov/index.php/?section=corporations

Hawaii $50 $50

http://cca.hawaii.gov/

Idaho $100 $100

http://www.sos.idaho.gov/corp/corindex.htm

Illinois $175 $500

http://www.cyberdriveillinois.com/departments/business_services/home.
html

Indiana $90 $90

http://www.in.gov/sos/business/3672.htm

Iowa $50 $100

http://sos.iowa.gov/

Kansas $90 $165
http://www.kssos.org/business/business_entity.html

Kentucky $50 $40
http://www.sos.ky.gov/bus/Pages/default.aspx

Louisiana $80 $105
http://www.sos.la.gov/BusinessServices/Pages/default.aspx

Maine $145 $175
http://www.maine.gov/sos/cec/corp/

Maryland $125 $105
http://www.dat.state.md.us/sdatweb/charter.html

Massachusetts $275 $520
http://www.sec.state.ma.us/cor/coridx.htm

Michigan $60 $50
http://www.michigan.gov/som/0,1607,7-192-29943_31408---,00.html

Minnesota $155 $155
http://www.sos.state.mn.us/index.aspx?page=1175

Mississippi $50 $50
https://corp.sos.ms.gov/corp/portal/c/page/corpBusinessIdSearch/portal.
aspx?#clear=1

Missouri	$58	$50

http://business.mo.gov/

Montana	$75	$75

http://sos.mt.gov/Business/index.asp

Nebraska	$65	$115

http://www.sos.ne.gov/business/

Nevada	$400	$400

http://nvsos.gov/index.aspx?page=243

New Hampshire	$100	$100

http://www.sos.nh.gov/corporate/index.html

New Jersey	$125	$125

http://www.nj.gov/treasury/revenue/

New Mexico	$100	$50

http://www.sos.state.nm.us/Business_Services/Corporations_Overview.a
spx

New York	$135	$200

http://www.dos.ny.gov/corps/

North Carolina	$125	$125
http://www.secretary.state.nc.us/corporations/		

North Dakota	$100	$135
http://sos.nd.gov/business/business-services		

Ohio	$125	$125
http://www.sos.state.oh.us/SOS/Businesses.aspx		

Oklahoma	$50	$100
https://www.sos.ok.gov/business/default.aspx		

Oregon	$100	$100
http://sos.oregon.gov/business/Pages/default.aspx		

Pennsylvania	$125	$125
http://www.dos.state.pa.us/portal/server.pt/community/corporation_bureau/12457		

Rhode Island	$230	$150
http://sos.ri.gov/business/		

South Carolina	$345	$110
http://www.scsos.com/Business_Filings		

South Dakota	$150	$150
http://www.sdsos.gov/busineservices/busineservices_overview.shtm		

Tennessee	$100	$300

http://www.state.tn.us/sos/bus_svc/index.htm

Texas	$310	$310

http://www.sos.state.tx.us/corp/index.shtml

Utah	$70	$70

http://corporations.utah.gov/

Vermont	$75	$125

https://www.sec.state.vt.us//corporations.aspx

Virginia	$75	$100

http://www.dba.virginia.gov/

Washington	$180	$180

http://www.sos.wa.gov/corps/

West Virginia	$50	$100

http://www.sos.wv.gov/business-licensing/Pages/default.aspx

Wisconsin	$100	$170

http://www.wdfi.org/corporations/

Wyoming	$100	$100

http://soswy.state.wy.us/Business/Default.aspx

Made in the USA
Columbia, SC
24 January 2024